D0717593

P • O • C • K • E • T • S

WORLD ATLAS

CZECH REPUBLIC

LAOS

PAKISTAN

JAMAICA

SAO TOME AND PRINCIPE

SOLOMON ISLANDS

CANADA

CHINA

Red R.

L Thac Ba

Black R.

Nam Ou

Thai Nguyen

Viet Tri

HANOI

Hong Gai

Hai Phong

Mekong

Mekong

Nam Dinh

Louang Phrabang

Thanh Hoa

Salween

LAOS

VIETNAM

Gulf of Tongking

Chiang Mai

Nam Theun

Vinh

VIENTIANE

Udon Thani

Muang Phitsanulok

P • O • C • K • E • T • S

WORLD ATLAS

Written by
ESTHER LABI

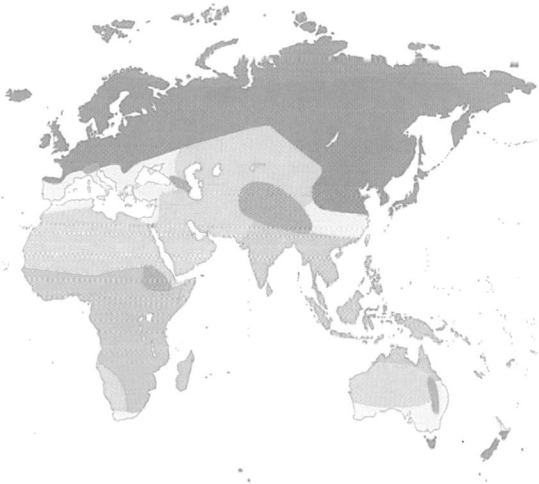

DORLING KINDERSLEY
London • New York • Moscow • Sydney
www.dk.com

A DORLING KINDERSLEY BOOK
www.dk.com

Editor Esther Labi
Designer Carlton Hibbert
Senior editor Hazel Egerton
Senior art editor Jacquie Gulliver
Editorial consultant Joan Dear
Picture research Lorna Ainger
Production Ruth Cobb

First published in Great Britain in 1995
by Dorling Kindersley Limited
9 Henrietta Street, London WC2E 8PS

2 4 6 8 10 9 7 5 3 1

Copyright © 1995 Dorling Kindersley Ltd., London
Revised edition 1997

All rights reserved. No part of this publication may be reproduced, stored in a retrieval system, or transmitted by any means, electronic, photocopying, recording, or otherwise, without the prior permission of the copyright owner.

A CIP catalogue record for this book is available from the British Library

ISBN 0 7513 3028 0

Colour reproduction by Colourscan, Singapore
Printed and bound in Italy by L.E.G.O.

CONTENTS

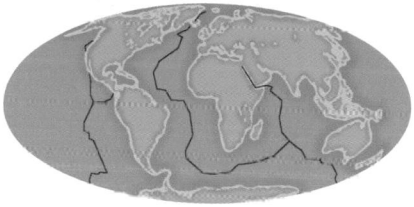

How to use this book 8
Guide to map pages 10
The planet Earth 12
The moving crust 14
Climate and vegetation 16
World time zones 18

NORTH AMERICA 20
Alaska and western Canada 22
Eastern Canada 24
Northeastern states 26
Southern states 28
The Great Lakes 30
Central and mountain states 32
Southwestern states 34
Pacific states 36
Mexico 38

CENTRAL AND SOUTH AMERICA 40
Central America and the Caribbean 42
Northern South America 44
Brazil 46
Southern South America 48
The Arctic and the Antarctic 50
The Atlantic Ocean 52

EUROPE 54
Scandinavia and Finland 56
The British Isles 58
Spain and Portugal 60
France 62
The Low Countries 64
Germany 66
Switzerland and Austria 68
Central Europe 70
Italy and Malta 72
South Central Europe 74
Southeast Europe 76
Greece 78
The Baltic States and Belorussia 80
European Russia 82
Ukraine and the Caucasus 84

AFRICA 86
Northwest Africa 88
Northeast Africa 90
West Africa 92

Central Africa 94
Central East Africa 96
Southern Africa 98
The Indian Ocean 100

NORTH AND WEST ASIA 102
Turkey and Cyprus 104
The Near East 106
The Middle East 108
Central Asia 110
The Russian Federation and Kazakhstan 112

SOUTH AND EAST ASIA 114
The Indian subcontinent 116
China and Mongolia 118
China and Korea 120
Japan 122
Mainland Southeast Asia 124
Maritime Southeast Asia 126
The Pacific Ocean 128

AUSTRALASIA 130
Australia and Papua New Guinea 132
New Zealand 134

Index 136

How to use this book

These pages show you how to use *Pockets: World Atlas*. The maps are organized by continent: North America, Central and South America, Europe, Africa, North and West Asia, South and East Asia, and Australasia. There is also an introductory section at the front and a comprehensive index at the back.

Key to icons

All the icons used in the Atlas are listed below.

The Arts

Climate

Communications

Environment

Flora and fauna

History

Industry

Natural features

People

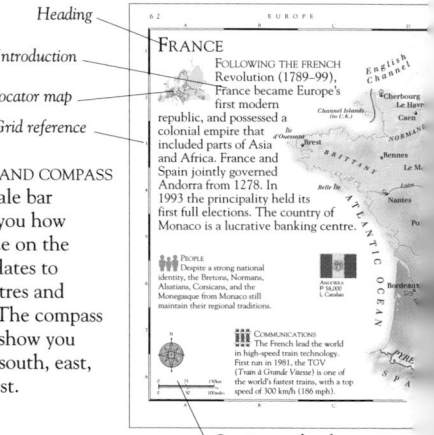

Scale and compass

The scale bar shows you how distance on the map relates to kilometres and miles. The compass points show you north, south, east, and west.

Locator map

This small map shows you the location of each country in relation to the continent to which it belongs.

Captions

These provide important information about each country, covering a variety of subjects such as the environment, people, climate, and history.

INTRODUCTION
This provides you with an overview of the area or region and gives interesting facts about the country's climate, landscape, and political situation.

RUNNING HEADS
These remind you which section you are in. At the top of the left-hand page is the name of the continent. The right-hand page gives the country. This page on France is in the section on Europe.

Running head

Caption icon

Caption

FLAGS
The flag of each nation is positioned next to the country. Also included are population figures (P) and information about the official languages spoken in that area (L).

Flag

GRID REFERENCE
The letters and numbers around this grid help you to locate places listed in the index. See page 136 for an explanation on how to use this grid.

GAZETTEER INDEX
A gazetteer index at the back of the book lists all the major towns, cities, rivers, mountain ranges, and lakes that appear in the book.

KEY TO MAPS

INTERNATIONAL BORDER

DISPUTED BORDER

STATE BORDER

CAPITAL CITY

STATE OR ADMINISTRATIVE CAPITAL

MAJOR TOWN

AIRPORT

SEAPORT

RIVER

CANAL

WADI

LAKE

SEASONAL LAKE

GUIDE TO MAP PAGES

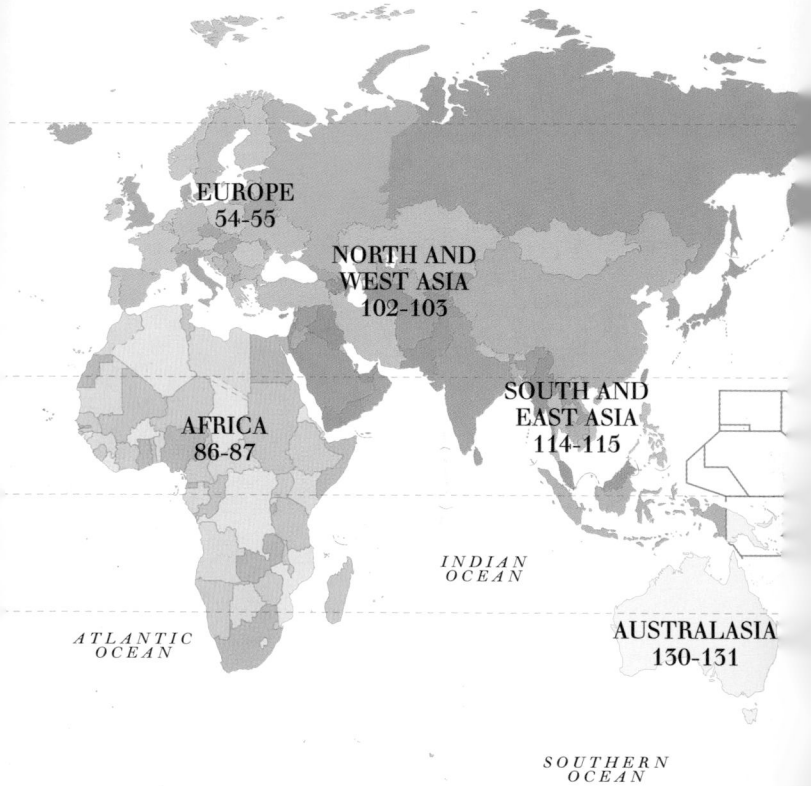

ARCTIC OCEAN
Arctic Circle
ATLANTIC OCEAN
NORTH AMERICA
20-21
PACIFIC OCEAN
Tropic of Cancer
Equator
CENTRAL AND SOUTH AMERICA
40-41
PACIFIC OCEAN
Tropic of Capricorn
ATLANTIC OCEAN

THE PLANET EARTH

EARTH, ONE OF nine planets that travel around the Sun, is part of the solar system within a galaxy called the Milky Way. The only planet within our solar system that supports life, Earth has sufficient light, heat, and water to support a wide range of plants and animals. The atmosphere protects the planet by filtering the Sun's rays.

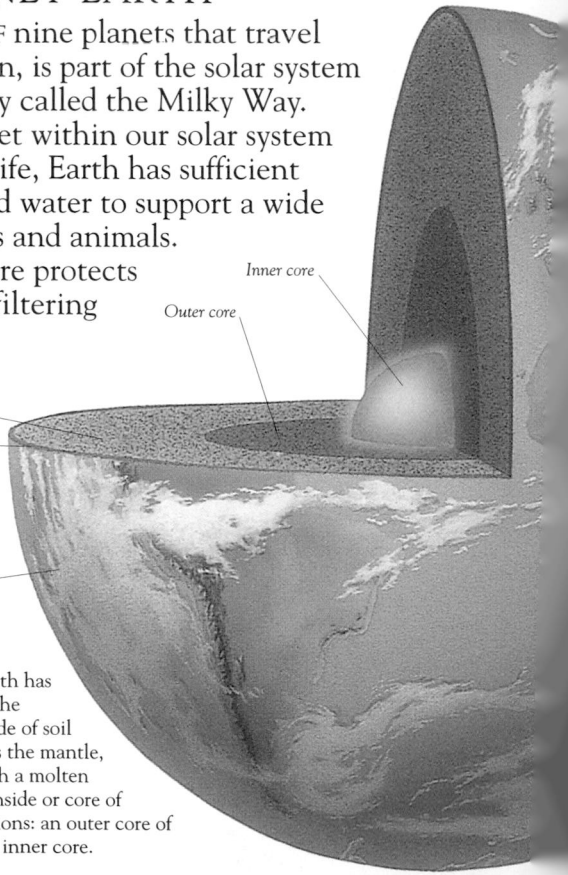

EARTH'S STRUCTURE
The interior of the Earth has four major layers. On the outside is the crust made of soil and rock. Under this is the mantle, which is solid rock with a molten layer at the top. The inside or core of the Earth has two sections: an outer core of thick fluid, and a solid inner core.

THE MOON

A ball of barren rock, the Moon orbits the Earth every 27.3 days. The Moon's gravity exerts a powerful pull on Earth. The Moon and Sun together create tides in the Earth's oceans. The highest tides occur twice a month when the Moon, Sun, and Earth are aligned.

Craters are caused by meteor collisions

EARTH'S ROTATION

Every 23 hours, 56 minutes, and 4 seconds the Earth rotates once on its axis. It turns towards the Sun and then away from it, causing day and night. The Earth's tilt produces days of different lengths. Seasons are caused by each hemisphere leaning towards and away from the Sun on the Earth's 365.242-day orbit.

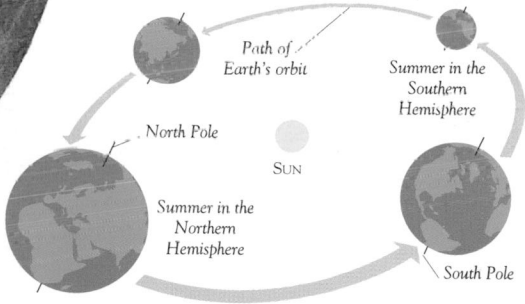

THE MOVING CRUST

THE EARTH'S CRUST is broken up into 15 plates in which the continents are embedded. Some countries lie in the middle of a plate, while others have a plate boundary through them. Forces in the Earth's mantle move the plates slowly around the globe, a process called continental drift. Rift valleys, ocean trenches, and mountains have all formed in areas where plates meet.

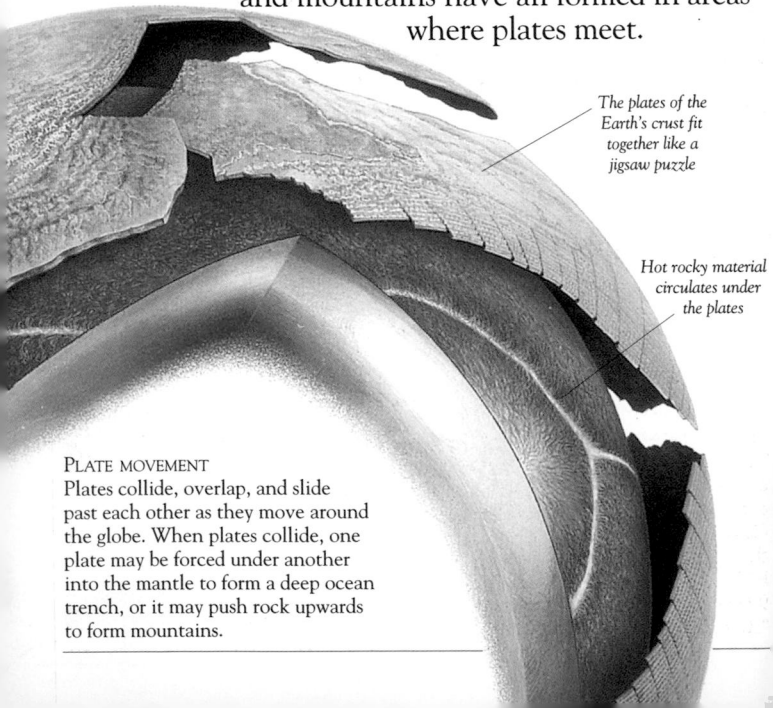

PLATE MOVEMENT
Plates collide, overlap, and slide past each other as they move around the globe. When plates collide, one plate may be forced under another into the mantle to form a deep ocean trench, or it may push rock upwards to form mountains.

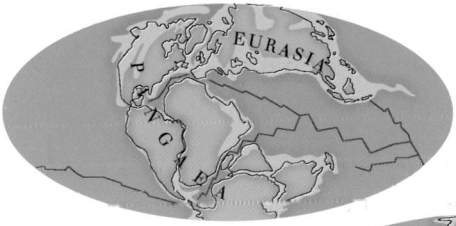

220 MILLION YEARS AGO
Scientists believe that about 220 million years ago the world's continents were part of one giant continent called Pangaea. Over the following 20 million years, it split into Laurasia and Gondwanaland.

100 MILLION YEARS AGO
Africa and South America separated 100 million years ago, breaking away from Antarctica. The Atlantic Ocean was created by a spreading ridge between North America, Europe, and Africa.

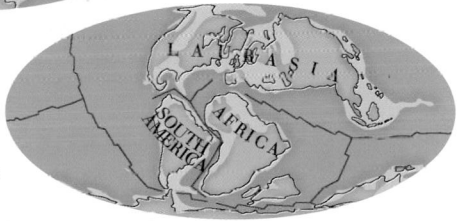

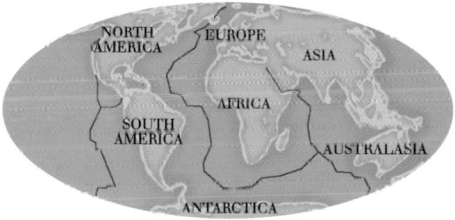

PRESENT DAY
Scientists can only guess what the world was like before Pangaea, but if the movement of plates continues, the Great Rift Valley will become an island and Africa and Europe will fuse.

SLIDING PLATES
The San Andreas fault, where two plates are sliding past each other, extends for 965 km (600 miles) in California, U.S.A. Movement between the plates is not steady and pressure builds up, causing earthquakes. About 90 per cent of earthquakes occur in the "Ring of Fire", around the Pacific plate.

CLIMATE AND VEGETATION

THE MAIN INFLUENCES on an area's climate are its distance from a large body of water, its height above sea level, and the amount of sunlight it receives. Rainfall and sunlight levels are highest at the equator, where the habitats with the most plant and animal life are found: rainforests, mangrove swamps, and coral reefs.

The world's largest remaining rainforest is in the Amazon Basin, Brazil

POLAR
Polar regions are so cold that few plants can survive. The treeless tundra regions of Siberia, Canada, Scandinavia, and Alaska support moss and lichens, as well as small flowers and shrubs during summer.

COOL
Coastal areas have less extreme climates than inland regions. Coniferous forests grow in cold northern Asia and North America. Warmer areas have forests of deciduous trees, which lose their leaves in winter.

WARM
Hot, dry summers and wet winters are typical of the Mediterranean region as well as parts of Southern Africa, the Americas, and Australia. Vegetation varies from treeless grasslands to open forests of trees and shrubs.

Desert and dry lands

Arid and semi-arid lands cover more than 30 per cent of the Earth's land surface. Semi-arid regions scattered with grasses and scrubs are called savannah. Cold deserts, like the ice deserts of the Arctic and Antarctic, have no more rain than the Sahara.

Tropical

High temperatures and high rainfall are typical of the Tropics. The main difference between tropical and monsoon climates is the distribution of rainfall. Tropical rainforests near the equator depend on year-round rainfall.

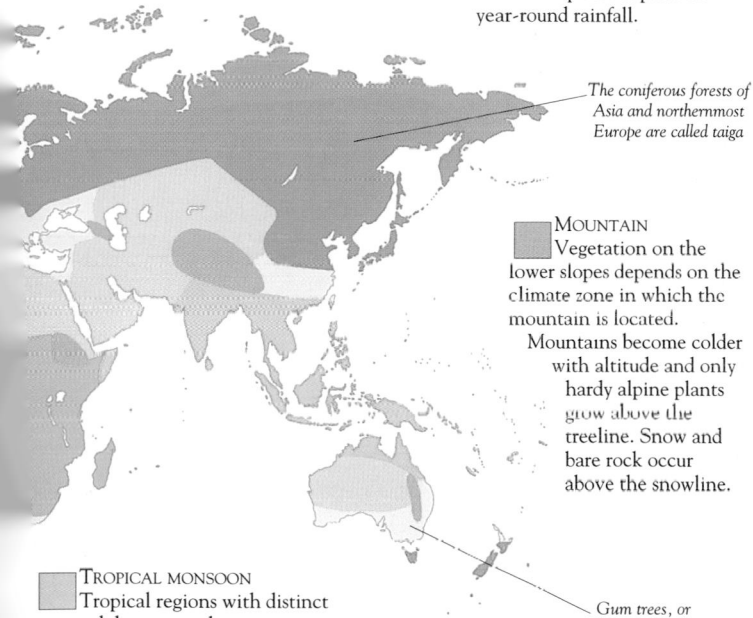

The coniferous forests of Asia and northernmost Europe are called taiga

Mountain

Vegetation on the lower slopes depends on the climate zone in which the mountain is located.

Mountains become colder with altitude and only hardy alpine plants grow above the treeline. Snow and bare rock occur above the snowline.

Gum trees, or Eucalyptus, have adapted to dry conditions

Tropical monsoon

Tropical regions with distinct wet and dry seasons have a monsoon climate. Each year, the monsoon winds reverse their direction completely, forming the two seasons.

WORLD TIME ZONES

IMAGINARY LINES are drawn around the globe, either parallel to the equator (latitude) or from pole to pole (longitude, or meridians). The Earth is divided into 24 time zones, one for each hour of the day. Greenwich is on 0° meridian and time advances by one hour for every 15° of longitude east of Greenwich.

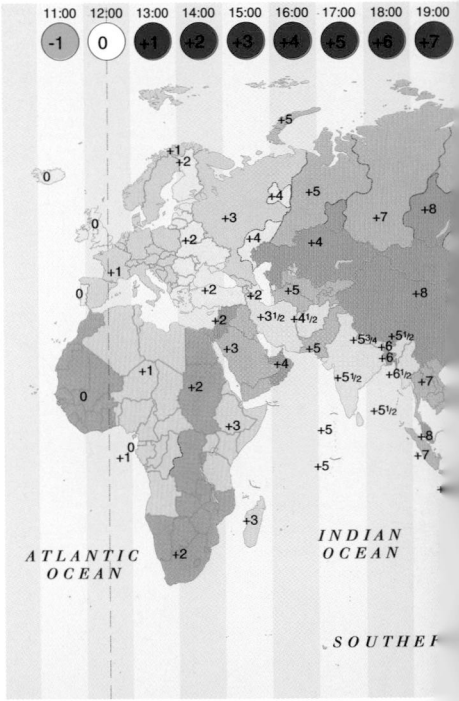

TIME ZONES

The numbers on the map indicate the number of hours which must be subtracted or added to reach GMT. When it is noon at Greenwich, for example, it is 11 p.m. in Sydney, Australia. Time zones are adjusted to regional administrative boundaries.

KEY TO MAP

- MINUS HOURS
- PLUS HOURS
- GREENWICH MEAN TIME
- DATE LINE
- TIME ZONES

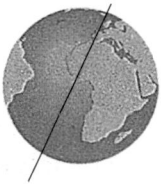

GMT

Greenwich Mean Time (GMT) is the time in Greenwich, England. Clocks are set depending on whether they are east or west of Greenwich.

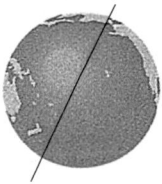

INTERNATIONAL DATE LINE

The International Date Line is an imaginary line that runs along the 180° meridian but deviates around countries.

21:00 22:00 23:00 24:00 01:00 02:00 03:00 04:00 05:00 06:00 07:00 08:00 09:00 10:00

+9 +10 +11 +12 -11 -10 -9 -8 -7 -6 -5 -4 -3 -2 -1

ARCTIC OCEAN

International Date Line

PACIFIC OCEAN

ATLANTIC OCEAN

PACIFIC OCEAN

ATLANTIC OCEAN

NORTH AMERICA

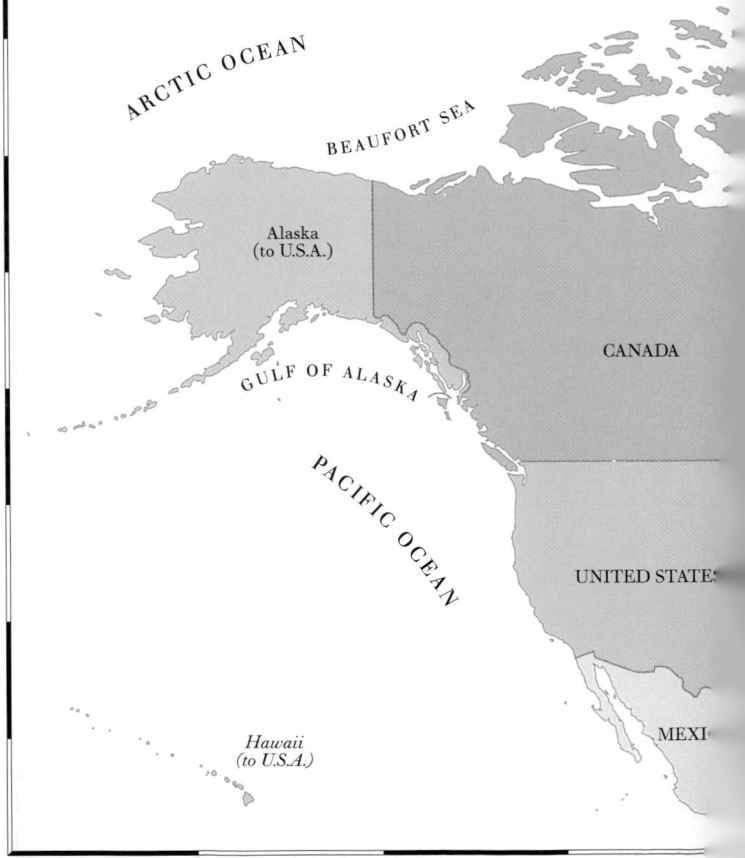

NORTH AMERICA

Canada and the United States of America make up most of the continent. To the south of the United States lie Mexico and Central America. The northernmost part of the continent sits in the Arctic Circle. Greenland, to the northeast of Canada, is the largest island in the world.

ALASKA AND WESTERN CANADA

AT THE END OF the last ice age, people travelled from Asia into North America over the Bering landbridge, which connected the continents at present-day Alaska.

ALASKA
P 550,043
L English

INDUSTRY
Fishing, oil, minerals, timber. Railways were the key to the development of farming in western Canada. The U.S.A.'s biggest oil field is at Prudhoe Bay, Alaska.

CLIMATE
A polar climate prevails in the north; the south is warmer. The Pacific coast, near Vancouver, has the warmest winters, and temperatures rarely fall below freezing.

HISTORY
The U.S.A. bought Alaska from Russia in 1867 for $7.2 million. Many Americans thought this was a waste of money until gold was discovered there in 1896 and oil in 1968.

ARCTIC OCEAN
Bering Strait
Prudhoe Bay
BEAUFOR
BROOKS RANGE
St. Lawrence I.
Aleutian Islands
Nunivak I.
St. Matthew I.
Yukon
BERING SEA
ALASKA (U.S.A.)
Porcupine
Fairbanks
YUKON TERRITORY
Umnak I.
Unalaska I.
Unimak I.
Bristol Bay
ALASKA RANGE
Yukon
Dawson
Anchorage
ROCKY MOUN
Kodiak I.
Gulf of Alaska
WHITEHORSE
JUNEAU
PACIFIC OCEAN
Queen Charlotte Is.
BRITI COLUM
Vancouver
Vancou
VICTO

WESTERN CANADA
P 7.99 million
L English, French

PEOPLE
The Inuit arrived in the area about 5,000 years ago. In 1999, the Northwest Territories became the self-governing Nunavut Territory, making the Inuit the first native North American people to gain independence.

FLORA AND FAUNA
Alaskan wildlife includes fur seals, moose, caribou, and many kinds of bear, including the kodiak, or Alaskan brown bear – the world's largest carnivorous land mammal.

Nares Strait
Ellesmere I.
Axel Heiberg I.
Queen Elizabeth Islands
Baffin Bay
Devon I.
Melville I.
McClure Strait
Banks I.
Parry Sound
Lancaster Sound
Somerset I.
Prince of Wales I.
Davis Strait
Baffin I.
Gulf of Boothia
Victoria I.
Amundsen Gulf
King William I.
Foxe Basin
Iqaluit
Hudson Strait
NORTHWEST TERRITORIES
Great Bear L.
Southampton I.
YELLOWKNIFE
Great Slave L.
Hudson Bay
NADA
L. Athabasca
Churchill
Fort McMurray
Churchill
Nelson
Athabasca
MANITOBA
ALBERTA
EDMONTON
L. Winnipeg
SASKATCHEWAN
Saskatoon
L. Winnipegosis
ONTARIO
Calgary
REGINA
WINNIPEG
TED STATES OF AMERICA

0 400 800km
0 200 400miles

EASTERN CANADA

ALTHOUGH IT IS the second largest country in the world, Canada has a relatively small population. Most people live within 160 km (100 miles) of the U.S. border. Snowbound for most of the year, the Hudson Bay area is a wilderness of forests, rivers, and lakes.

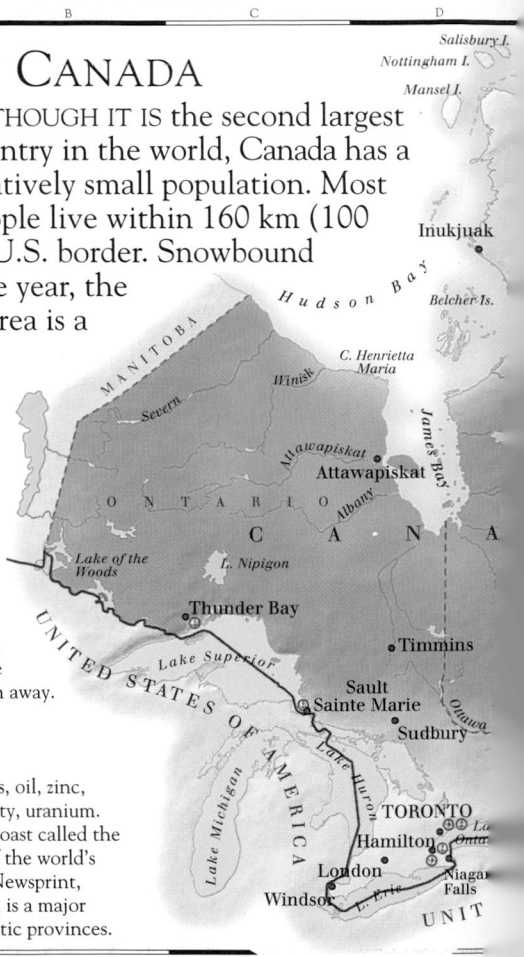

PEOPLE
The Vikings were the first Europeans to visit eastern Canada in about 986 B.C. They settled for only a short time before the Native Americans drove them away.

INDUSTRY
Wood industries, oil, zinc, nickel, hydro-electricity, uranium. The area off the east coast called the Grand Banks is one of the world's richest fishing areas. Newsprint, made from wood pulp, is a major export from the Atlantic provinces.

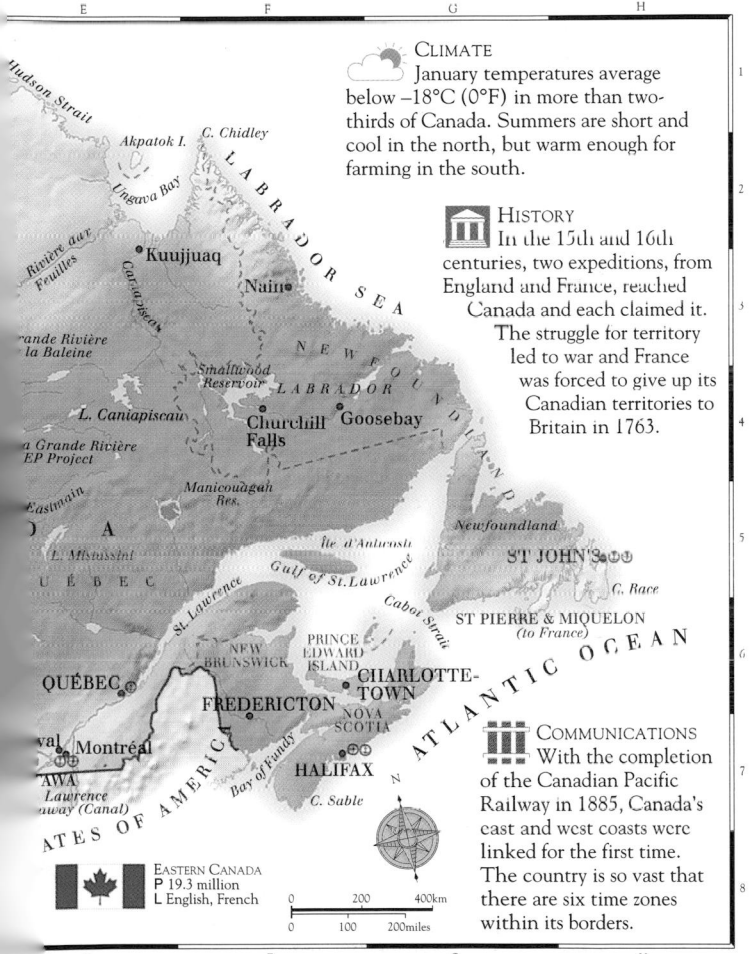

CLIMATE

January temperatures average below –18°C (0°F) in more than two-thirds of Canada. Summers are short and cool in the north, but warm enough for farming in the south.

HISTORY

In the 15th and 16th centuries, two expeditions, from England and France, reached Canada and each claimed it. The struggle for territory led to war and France was forced to give up its Canadian territories to Britain in 1763.

COMMUNICATIONS

With the completion of the Canadian Pacific Railway in 1885, Canada's east and west coasts were linked for the first time. The country is so vast that there are six time zones within its borders.

NORTHEASTERN STATES

WITH ITS RICH MINERAL resources and safe harbours, northeast America was the first area on the continent to be colonized by Europeans. In 1620, English pilgrims sailed on the *Mayflower* to settle in a region that is still called New England. During the mid-19th century, European immigrants settled in New York City and in other East Coast cities. Today, this region is the most densely populated and heavily industrialized area of the U.S.A.

CLIMATE

This area of the U.S.A. has a temperate climate, with warm and humid summers. However, the northeastern region, in particular, can experience very heavy snowfall from November to April.

NORTHEASTERN STATES
P 51.5 million
L English

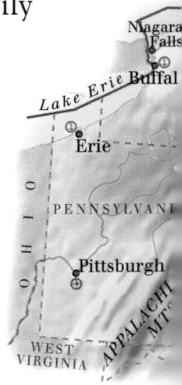

PEOPLE

Northeastern Native American tribes, such as the Wampanoag, the Algonquin, and the tribes of the Iroquois League, were the first to come into contact with European settlers and explorers.

INDUSTRY

Oil, iron, steel, chemicals, maple sugar, blueberries, cranberries, fishing, tourism. Vermont is the main producer of maple syrup in the U.S.A. The stock exchange on Wall Street, New York City, is the largest in the world.

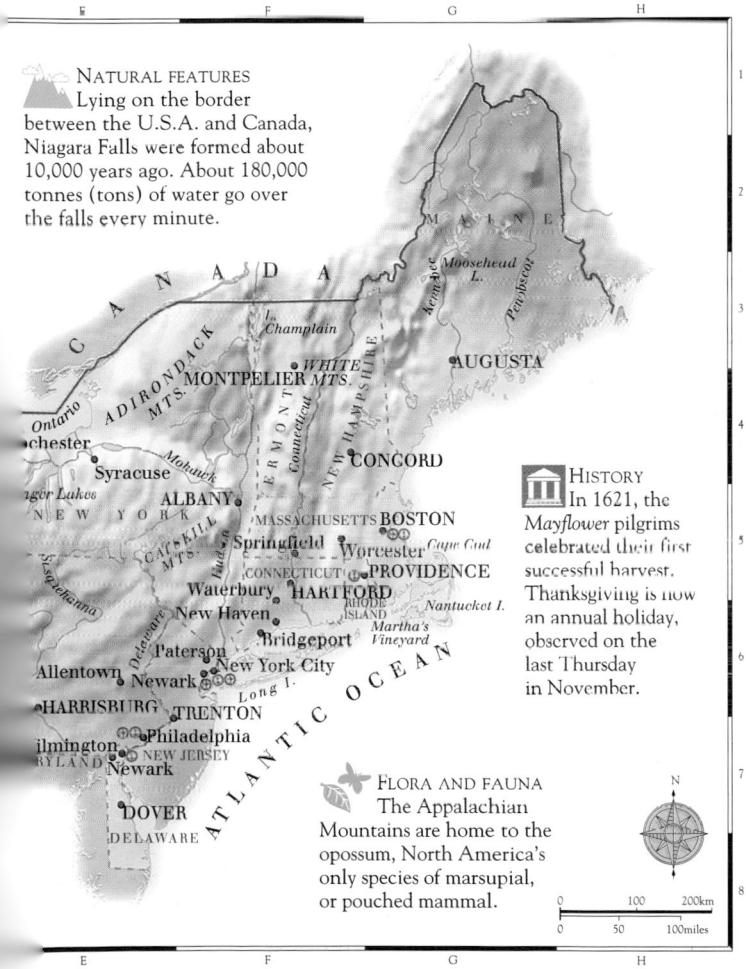
E
F
G
H
1
2
3
4
5
6
7
8
NATURAL FEATURES
Lying on the border between the U.S.A. and Canada, Niagara Falls were formed about 10,000 years ago. About 180,000 tonnes (tons) of water go over the falls every minute.
HISTORY
In 1621, the *Mayflower* pilgrims celebrated their first successful harvest. Thanksgiving is now an annual holiday, observed on the last Thursday in November.
FLORA AND FAUNA
The Appalachian Mountains are home to the opossum, North America's only species of marsupial, or pouched mammal.
CANADA
MAINE
Moosehead L.
Kennebec
Penobscot
AUGUSTA
L. Champlain
ADIRONDACK MTS.
MONTPELIER
WHITE MTS.
VERMONT
Connecticut
NEW HAMPSHIRE
CONCORD
Ontario
Syracuse
Mohawk
ALBANY
NEW YORK
MASSACHUSETTS
BOSTON
CATSKILL MTS.
Hudson
Springfield
Worcester
Cape Cod
CONNECTICUT
PROVIDENCE
Waterbury
HARTFORD
RHODE ISLAND
Nantucket I.
Susquehanna
Delaware
New Haven
Martha's Vineyard
Bridgeport
Paterson
New York City
Allentown
Newark
Long I.
HARRISBURG
TRENTON
Philadelphia
NEW JERSEY
Newark
DOVER
DELAWARE
ATLANTIC OCEAN
N
0 100 200km
0 50 100miles

SOUTHERN STATES

BY THE 19TH CENTURY, the wealth of the South was based on crops like tobacco, indigo, rice, and especially cotton, which was grown on large plantations by African slaves. The area is known today for New Orleans' jazz, Florida's Disney World, and the Kentucky Derby. The city of Washington, in the District of Columbia, was made the U.S. capital in 1800.

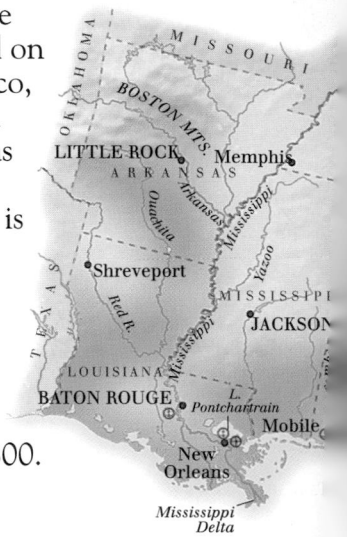

CLIMATE
Summers are long and hot; winters are mild, but temperatures are generally warmer on the coast than inland. Southern Florida is tropical.

INDUSTRY
Soya beans, coal, peanuts, cotton, citrus fruits, tobacco, oil, tourism. Georgia grows half of the U.S.A's peanuts – most are used to make peanut butter.

THE ARTS
The French brought Mardi Gras to America in the early 1700 Celebrated in many of the souther states, the most famous festival is held in New Orleans. Here parade last for a week before Mardi Gras Day, the day before Lent starts.

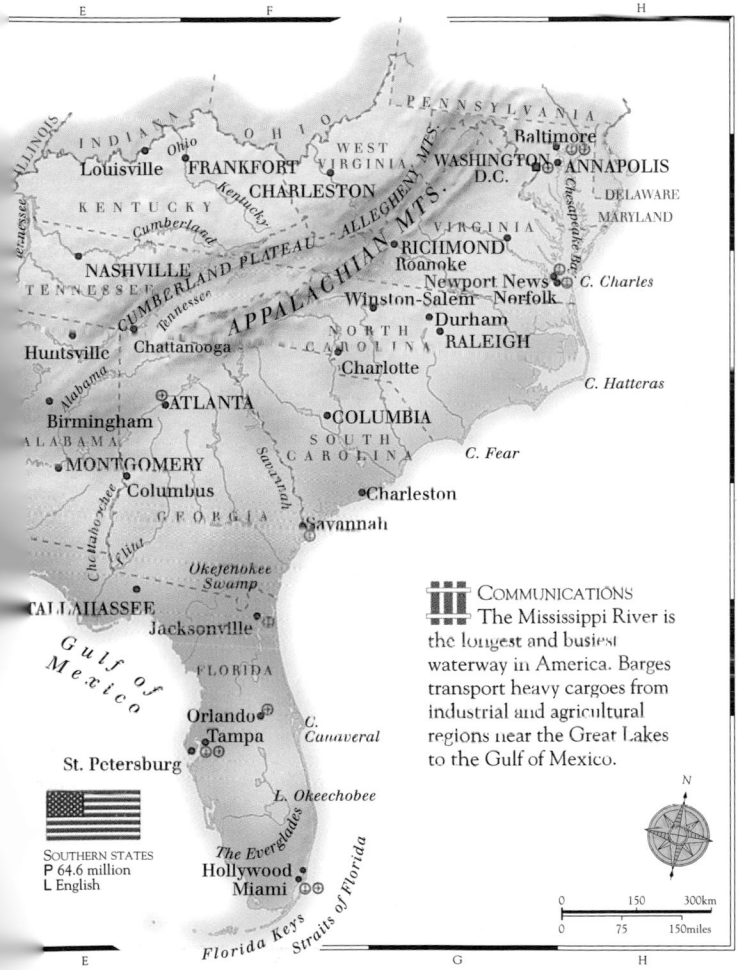

COMMUNICATIONS
The Mississippi River is the longest and busiest waterway in America. Barges transport heavy cargoes from industrial and agricultural regions near the Great Lakes to the Gulf of Mexico.

THE GREAT LAKES

THE STATES OF Indiana, Illinois, Michigan, Ohio, Wisconsin, and Minnesota, which all border on one or more of the five Great Lakes, are often called the industrial and agricultural heartland of the United States. The region is rich in natural resources, with large areas of fertile farmland on flat plains called prairies.

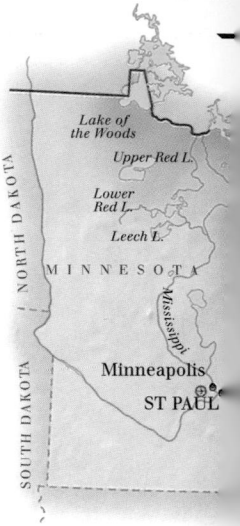

CLIMATE

The region around the Great Lakes has warm summers but quite severe winters, and parts of the lakes can freeze over. Minnesota, in particular, suffers from heavy snowstorms.

GREAT LAKES STATES
P 46.4 million
L English

ENVIRONMENT

The Great Lakes – Ontario, Huron, Superior, Michigan, and Erie – together form the largest area of fresh water in the world. Heavy industry has caused severe water pollution, and in some areas it is dangerous to eat the fish or swim.

INDUSTRY

Vehicles, coal, iron, grain, maize, cherries.
Nearly half of the world's maize crop and a third of the cherry crop are grown in the Great Lakes region. Detroit is known as "motor city" because it is the centre of the U.S. car industry.

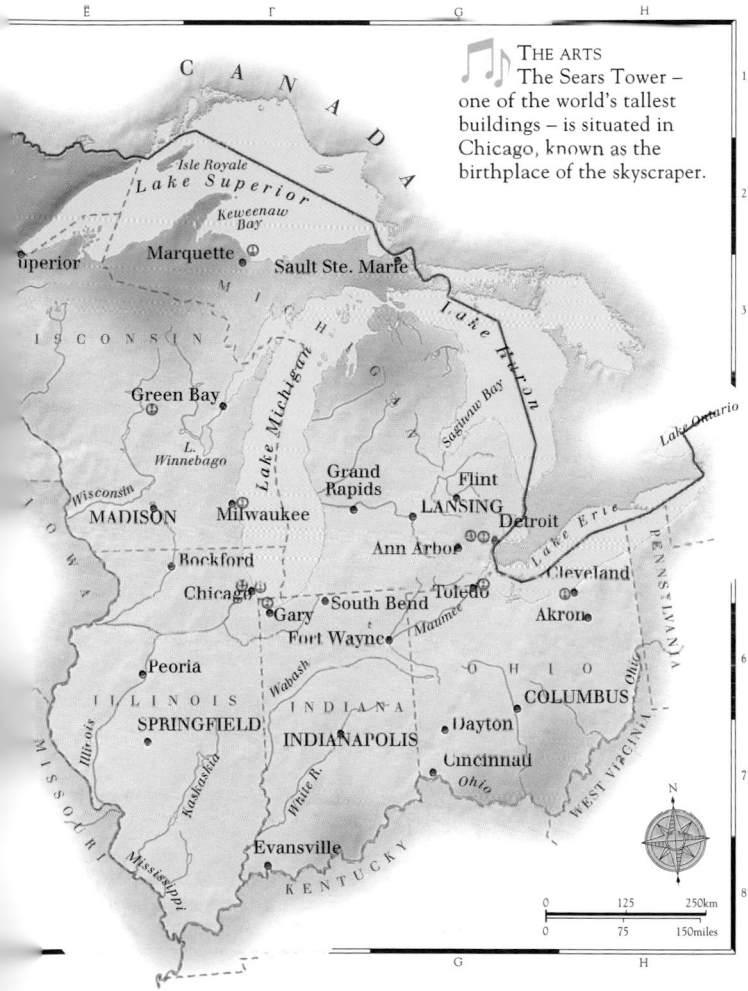
THE ARTS
The Sears Tower – one of the world's tallest buildings – is situated in Chicago, known as the birthplace of the skyscraper.
CANADA
Isle Royale
Lake Superior
Keweenaw Bay
Marquette
Sault Ste. Marie
Lake Huron
Green Bay
L. Winnebago
Lake Michigan
Saginaw Bay
Lake Ontario
Grand Rapids
Flint
LANSING
Detroit
Lake Erie
Wisconsin
MADISON
Milwaukee
Ann Arbor
Rockford
Cleveland
Chicago
Toledo
Gary
South Bend
Akron
Maumee
Fort Wayne
Peoria
Wabash
OHIO
COLUMBUS
ILLINOIS
INDIANA
SPRINGFIELD
INDIANAPOLIS
Dayton
Illinois
Kaskaskia
White R.
Cincinnati
Ohio
Evansville
Mississippi
KENTUCKY
WEST VIRGINIA
PENNSYLVANIA
MISSOURI
IOWA
0 125 250km
0 75 150miles

CENTRAL AND MOUNTAIN STATES

THE GREAT Plains, the Rocky Mountains, and the Mississippi lowlands dominate the landscape of the Midwest. Once home to Native Americans and herds of bison, the Great Plains were settled in the 19th century by Europeans, who forced the Native Americans onto reservations and slaughtered the bison to near extinction.

HISTORY

Pioneers travelling to the West had to cross the Great Plains, which were known as the "Great American Desert". The last area to be settled, it is now a wealthy agricultural region.

CENTRAL AND MOUNTAIN STATES
P 18.7 million
L English

CLIMATE

West of the Rockies, the summers are cooler and the winters are warmer. States on the Great Plains have an extreme climate, which can change quite suddenly and violently – blizzards, hail, thunderstorms, and tornadoes may occur.

NATURAL FEATURES

The Rocky Mountains exten through Canada and the U.S.A. for more than 4,800 km (3,000 miles). They divide North America and separate the rivers flowing west to the Pacific from those flowing east to the Atlantic.

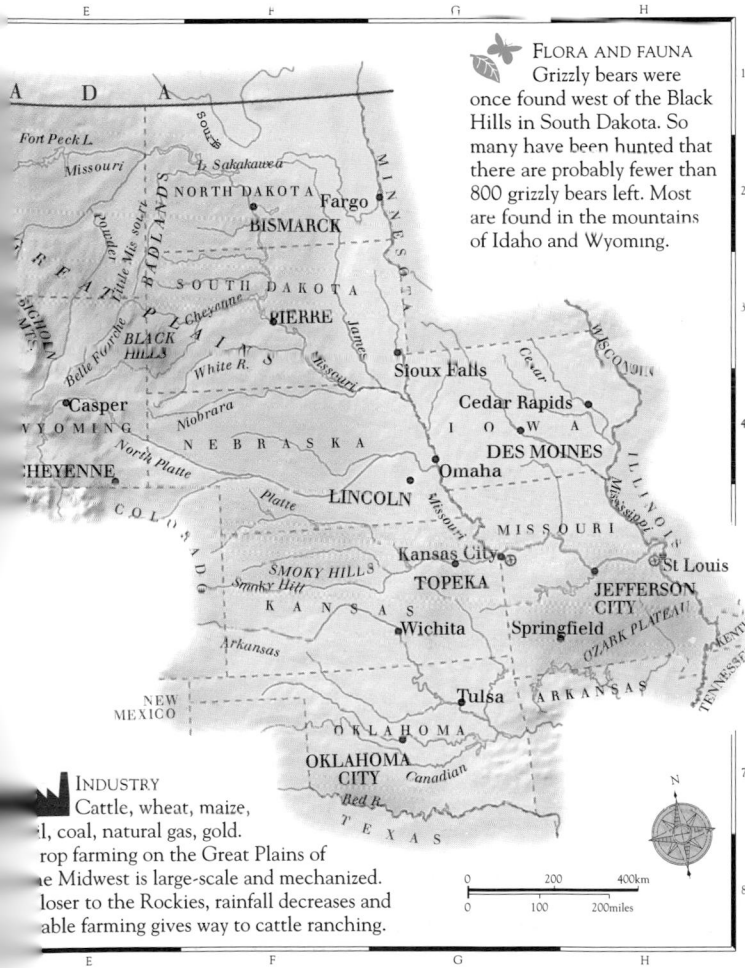

FLORA AND FAUNA
Grizzly bears were once found west of the Black Hills in South Dakota. So many have been hunted that there are probably fewer than 800 grizzly bears left. Most are found in the mountains of Idaho and Wyoming.

INDUSTRY
Cattle, wheat, maize,
l, coal, natural gas, gold.
rop farming on the Great Plains of
e Midwest is large-scale and mechanized.
loser to the Rockies, rainfall decreases and
able farming gives way to cattle ranching.

SOUTHWESTERN STATES

THE FIRST Europeans in the Southwest

were the Spanish, who travelled north from Mexico. This resulted in a mingling of Spanish and Native American cultures in the region. Gold and silver mining and cattle-ranching attracted other settlers in the late 19th century, when this area became part of the U.S.A. after the Mexican War.

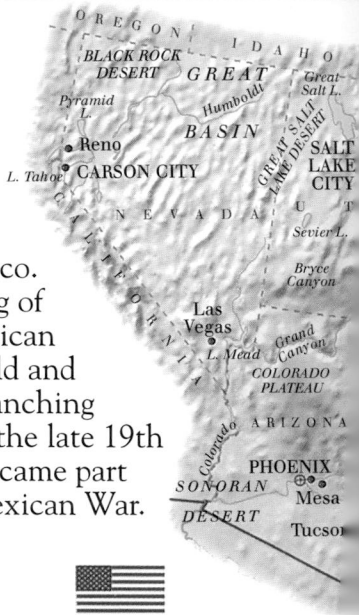

SOUTHWESTERN STATES
P 28.4 million
L English

NATURAL FEATURES

The Colorado plateau has some unusual landforms, including natural bridges and arches of solid rock. Over the past million years, the Colorado River has cut away the plateau, forming the world's largest river gorge – the Grand Canyon.

HISTORY

At the end of the Mexican War (1846–48), the U.S.A. acquired Utah, Nevada, California, and parts of Arizona, New Mexico, Colorado, and Wyoming. One of the causes of the war was a border dispute between Texas and Mexico.

PEOPLE

Some of the earliest Native Americans lived in the Nevada area. Bones and ashes discovered near Las Vegas indicate that people may have lived there more than 20,000 years ago. Today, the region has the largest concentration of Native Americans in the country.

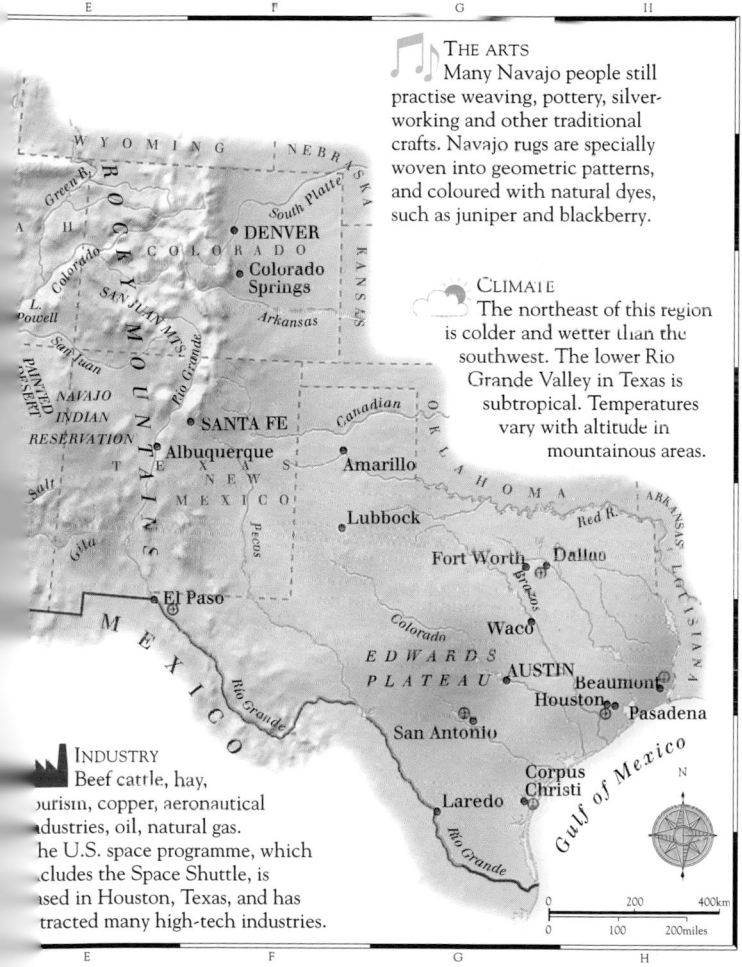

THE ARTS

Many Navajo people still practise weaving, pottery, silver-working and other traditional crafts. Navajo rugs are specially woven into geometric patterns, and coloured with natural dyes, such as juniper and blackberry.

CLIMATE

The northeast of this region is colder and wetter than the southwest. The lower Rio Grande Valley in Texas is subtropical. Temperatures vary with altitude in mountainous areas.

INDUSTRY

Beef cattle, hay, ourism, copper, aeronautical dustries, oil, natural gas. he U.S. space programme, which cludes the Space Shuttle, is sed in Houston, Texas, and has tracted many high-tech industries.

PACIFIC STATES

ALL THREE STATES on the West Coast are major agricultural producers – Washington and Oregon supply one-third of the softwood timber in the U.S. and California produces half of the country's fruit and vegetables. Situated where two of the Earth's plates meet, the area suffers from earthquakes and volcanic activity. Mount St. Helens, dormant since 1857, erupted in 1980, losing some 400 m (1,300 ft) off its height.

NATURAL FEATURES

The lowest point in the western hemisphere is in Death Valley, 86 m (282 ft) below sea level. One of the driest, hottest places on Earth, the highest temperature, 57°C (135°F), was recorded there in 1913, and its average rainfall is only 38 mm (1.5 in) per year.

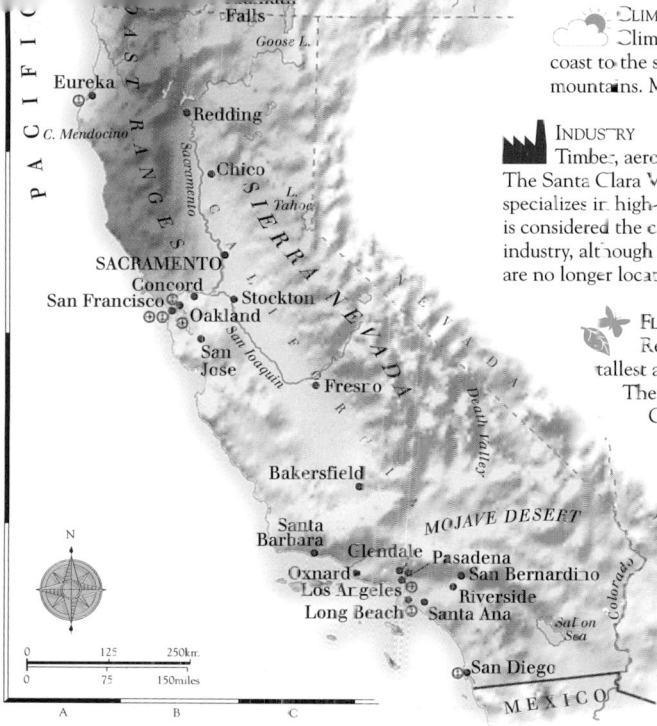

Climate

Climate varies from the moderate coast to the snow-capped Sierra Nevada mountains. Much of California is arid desert.

Industry

Timber, aerospace industries, wine. The Santa Clara Valley, or Silicon Valley, specializes in high-tech industry. Hollywood is considered the centre of the U.S. film industry, although many major studios are no longer located there.

Flora and Fauna

Redwoods are believed to be the tallest and oldest trees in the world. They are found along the West Coast from central California to southern Oregon and rarely occur more than 80 km (50 miles) inland.

Pacific States
P 37.5 million
L English

MEXICO

THE ANCIENT empires of the Maya and Aztec flourished for centuries before the Spanish invaded Mexico in 1519, lured there by legends of hoards of gold and silver. Mexico gained its independence in 1810, after 300 years of Spanish rule. Today, most Mexicans are *mestizo*, a mix of Spanish and Native American. Although Spanish is the official language, Native American languages such as Maya, Nahuatl, and Zapotec are also widely spoken.

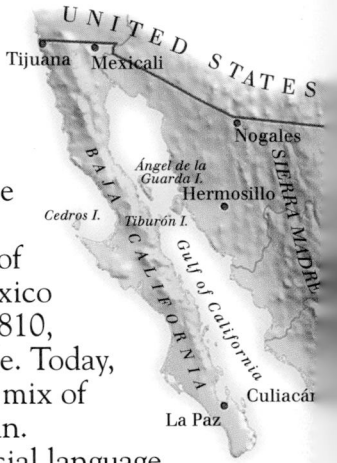

CLIMATE

The Mexican plateau and mountains are warm for most of the year. The Pacific coast has a tropical climate.

FLORA AND FAUNA

The Mexican beaded lizard and the gila monster are the only two poisonous lizards known. The largest of all cacti is the giant saguaro, which grows in the Sonora Desert to a height of more than 18 m (60 ft).

NATURAL FEATURES

The plateau of Mexico is enclosed to the west and east by the Sierra Madre mountain ranges, which occupy 75 per cent of the total land area. Mexico is so mountainous and arid in parts that only 12 per cent of the land is arable

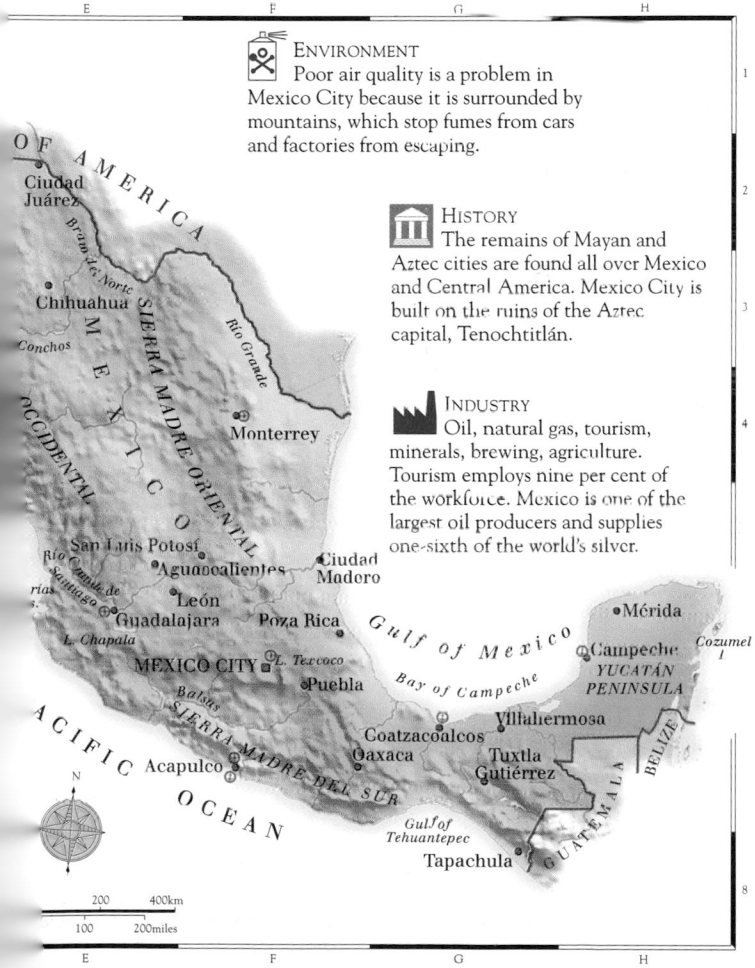

ENVIRONMENT
Poor air quality is a problem in Mexico City because it is surrounded by mountains, which stop fumes from cars and factories from escaping.

HISTORY
The remains of Mayan and Aztec cities are found all over Mexico and Central America. Mexico City is built on the ruins of the Aztec capital, Tenochtitlán.

INDUSTRY
Oil, natural gas, tourism, minerals, brewing, agriculture. Tourism employs nine per cent of the workforce. Mexico is one of the largest oil producers and supplies one-sixth of the world's silver.

CENTRAL AND SOUTH AMERICA
BAHAMAS
CUBA
JAMAICA
HAITI
DOMINICAN REPUBLIC
Puerto Rico (to U.S.A.)
ANTIGUA & BARBUDA
DOMINICA
ST. LUCIA
BARBADOS
ST. VINCENT & THE GRENADINES
GRENADA
TRINIDAD & TOBAGO
ST. KITTS & NEVIS
CARIBBEAN SEA
SURINAM
French Guiana (to France)
GUYANA
VENEZUELA
COLOMBIA
BRAZIL
PERU
ECUADOR
Galapagos Islands (to Ecuador)
PACIFIC
PANAMA
COSTA RICA
NICARAGUA
HONDURAS
BELIZE
GUATEMALA
EL SALVADOR

Central and South America

Until three million years ago, South America was an island with its own unique flora and fauna. The narrow Isthmus of Panama is the continent's only link to North America. South America's southernmost tip, Cape Horn, is only 970 km (600 miles) from Antarctica.

CENTRAL AMERICA AND THE CARIBBEAN

CENTRAL AMERICA FORMS a narrow land bridge linking North and South America. To the east lie the Caribbean islands, many of which are uninhabited.

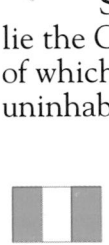

GUATEMALA
P 10 million
L Spanish

EL SALVADOR
P 5.4 million
L Spanish

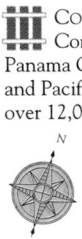

COMMUNICATIONS
Completed in 1914, the Panama Canal links the Atlantic and Pacific Oceans. Each year over 12,000 ships use the canal to avoid the long and treacherous route around Cape Horn.

HONDURAS
P 5.6 million
L Spanish

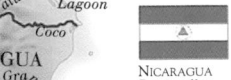

NICARAGUA
P 4.1 million
L Spanish

COSTA RICA
P 3.3 million
L Spanish

PANAMA
P 2.6 million
L Spanish

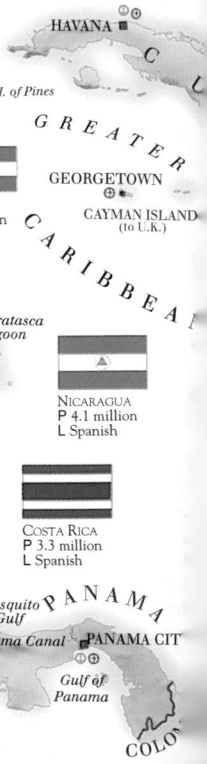

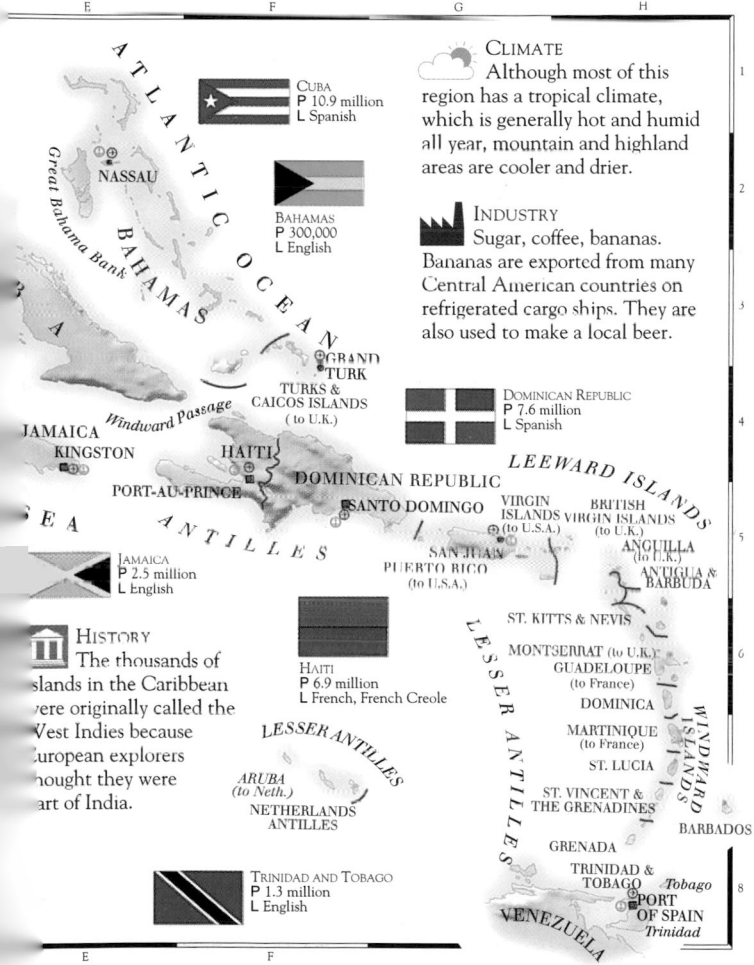
E
F
G
H
1
2
3
4
5
6
8
ATLANTIC OCEAN
Great Bahama Bank
NASSAU
BAHAMAS
GRAND TURK
TURKS & CAICOS ISLANDS (to U.K.)
Windward Passage
JAMAICA
KINGSTON
HAITI
PORT-AU-PRINCE
DOMINICAN REPUBLIC
SANTO DOMINGO
LEEWARD ISLANDS
VIRGIN ISLANDS (to U.S.A.)
BRITISH VIRGIN ISLANDS (to U.K.)
ANGUILLA (to U.K.)
ANTIGUA & BARBUDA
SAN JUAN
PUERTO RICO (to U.S.A.)
ANTILLES
ST. KITTS & NEVIS
MONTSERRAT (to U.K.)
GUADELOUPE (to France)
DOMINICA
MARTINIQUE (to France)
ST. LUCIA
ST. VINCENT & THE GRENADINES
GRENADA
TRINIDAD & TOBAGO
Tobago
PORT OF SPAIN
Trinidad
VENEZUELA
LESSER ANTILLES
WINDWARD ISLANDS
BARBADOS
LESSER ANTILLES
ARUBA (to Neth.)
NETHERLANDS ANTILLES
CUBA
P 10.9 million
L Spanish
BAHAMAS
P 300,000
L English
DOMINICAN REPUBLIC
P 7.6 million
L Spanish
JAMAICA
P 2.5 million
L English
HAITI
P 6.9 million
L French, French Creole
TRINIDAD AND TOBAGO
P 1.3 million
L English
CLIMATE
Although most of this region has a tropical climate, which is generally hot and humid all year, mountain and highland areas are cooler and drier.
INDUSTRY
Sugar, coffee, bananas. Bananas are exported from many Central American countries on refrigerated cargo ships. They are also used to make a local beer.
HISTORY
The thousands of islands in the Caribbean were originally called the West Indies because European explorers thought they were part of India.

NORTHERN SOUTH AMERICA

THE INCAS RULED MUCH of this area in the 15th century, and today large numbers of their descendants live in Peru, Ecuador, and Bolivia. In 1533, the last Incan emperor was executed by the Spanish, who colonized this region. The French, Dutch, and British later settled in the countries east of Venezuela, although all but French Guiana are now independent.

VENEZUELA
P 20.6 million
L Spanish

GUYANA
P 800,000
L English

SURINAM
P 400,000
L Dutch

CARIBBEAN SEA
Gulf of Venezuela
Barranquilla
Santa Marta
Cartagena
Maracaibo
Gulf of Darien
Barquisimeto
L. Maracaibo
CARACAS
Valencia
Margarita I.
Cumaná
Maturín
PANAMA
Cauca
Magdalena
Barinas
Mérida
Apure
Ciudad Bolívar
Orinoco
Ciudad Guayana
Arauca
VENEZUELA
Medellín
Meta
GEORGETOWN
New Amsterdam
PARAMARIBO
GUYANA
BOGOTÁ
Buenaventura
Villavicencio
SURINAM
CAYENNE
FRENCH GUIANA (to France)
Essequibo
Berbice
Courantyne
Marowijne
Cali
Guaviare
COLOMBIA
AMAZON BASIN

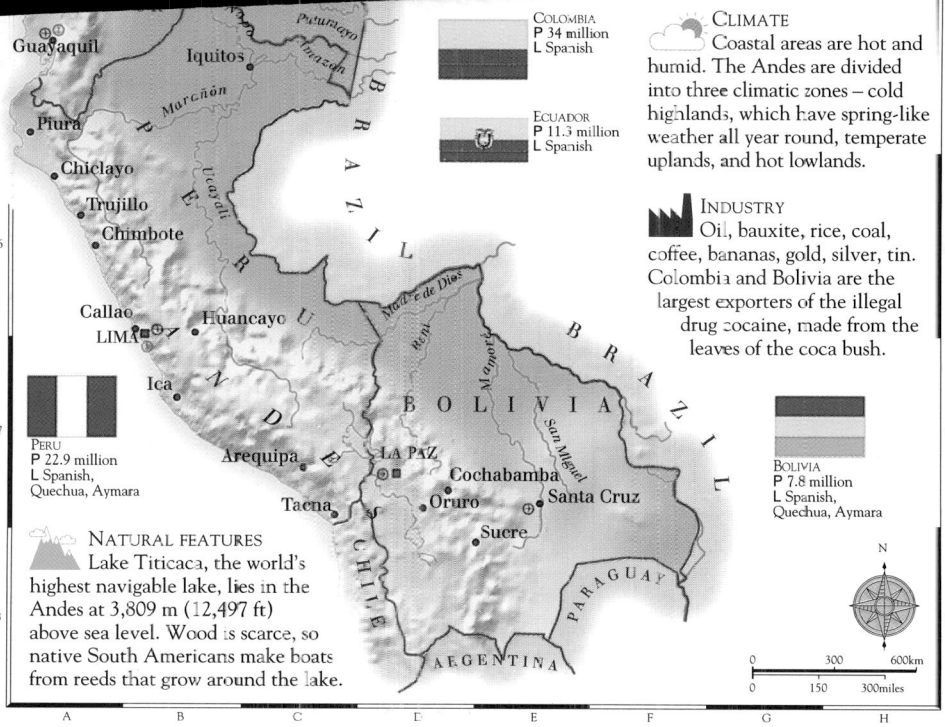

CLIMATE

Coastal areas are hot and humid. The Andes are divided into three climatic zones – cold highlands, which have spring-like weather all year round, temperate uplands, and hot lowlands.

INDUSTRY

Oil, bauxite, rice, coal, coffee, bananas, gold, silver, tin. Colombia and Bolivia are the largest exporters of the illegal drug cocaine, made from the leaves of the coca bush.

NATURAL FEATURES

Lake Titicaca, the world's highest navigable lake, lies in the Andes at 3,809 m (12,497 ft) above sea level. Wood is scarce, so native South Americans make boats from reeds that grow around the lake.

BRAZIL

OCCUPYING NEARLY HALF of South America, Brazil has the largest river basin in the world. Many Brazilians are descendants of Portuguese, who colonized Brazil in the 16th century, and Africans, who were brought to work on sugar plantations. Over the years, people have moved from the countryside in search of work, so that today almost 75 per cent of Brazilians live in cities. Chronic housing shortages mean about 25 million people live in sprawling shanty towns called *favelas*.

PEOPLE
There were once about two million indigenous people living in Amazonia. Today only 50,000 remain. The survival of many tribes and their way of life is threatened by the destruction of the Amazon rainforest.

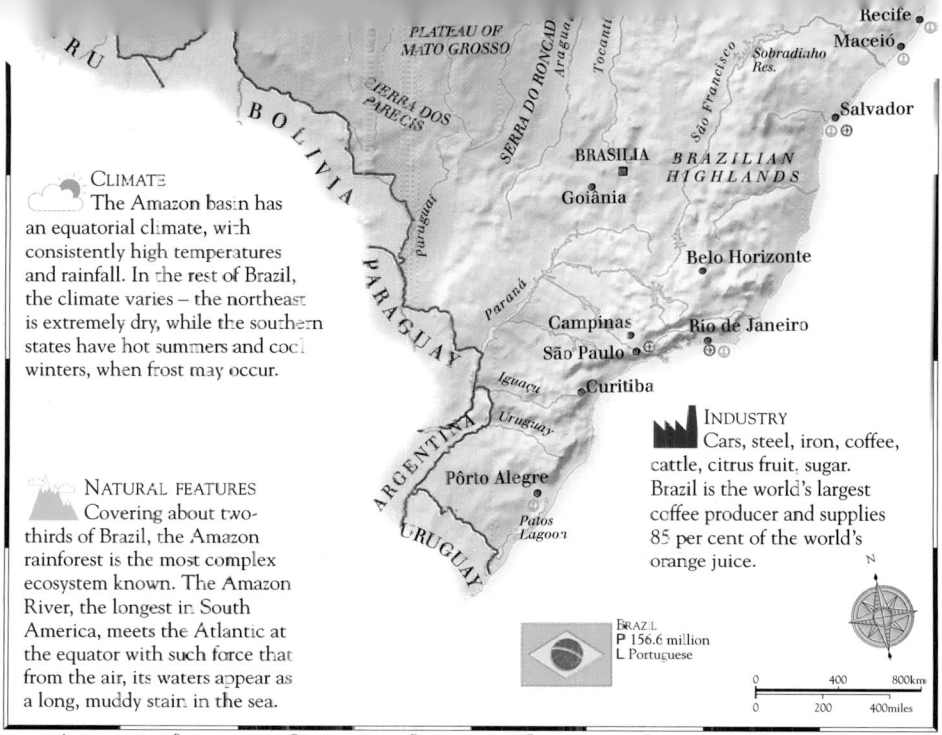

Climate

The Amazon basin has an equatorial climate, with consistently high temperatures and rainfall. In the rest of Brazil, the climate varies – the northeast is extremely dry, while the southern states have hot summers and cool winters, when frost may occur.

Natural features

Covering about two-thirds of Brazil, the Amazon rainforest is the most complex ecosystem known. The Amazon River, the longest in South America, meets the Atlantic at the equator with such force that from the air, its waters appear as a long, muddy stain in the sea.

Industry

Cars, steel, iron, coffee, cattle, citrus fruit, sugar. Brazil is the world's largest coffee producer and supplies 85 per cent of the world's orange juice.

Brazil
P 156.6 million
L Portuguese

SOUTHERN SOUTH AMERICA

THE LANDSCAPE OF this region of South America varies from snow-capped volcanoes in the Andes to the wastelands of Patagonia. In the heart of Argentina lie the Pampas, fertile grasslands where vast herds of cattle graze. In parts, grasses grow up to 3 m (10 ft) high. Chile is separated from the rest of the region by the Andes, which run the length of the continent.

CLIMATE
Paraguay is subtropical; farther south is temperate. The Andes have year-round snow, while parts of the Atacama desert in Chile have had no rain for 400 years.

INDUSTRY

Copper, wool, beef, wheat. Chile is the world's largest copper producer, and Uruguay is the second-largest wool exporter.

ARGENTINA
P 33.5 million
L Spanish

HISTORY

Before the discovery of Cape Horn at the tip of the continent in 1616, ships used the dangerous Straits of Magellan to travel between the Atlantic and the Pacific Oceans. Today, ships use the Panama Canal.

NATURAL FEATURES

The longest chain of mountains in the world, the Andes extend for 7,240 km (4,500 miles). They are the most recently formed mountains on Earth, and the area suffers from earthquakes and volcanic activity. Glaciers, fjords, lakes, and deep-sea channels are features of the southern Andes.

THE ANTARCTIC

CONTAINING 80 PERCENT of the world's freshwater, the continent of Antarctica lies buried under ice more than 2 km (1.2 miles) thick. The surrounding seas are partly frozen, and icebergs barricade over 90 percent of the coastline.

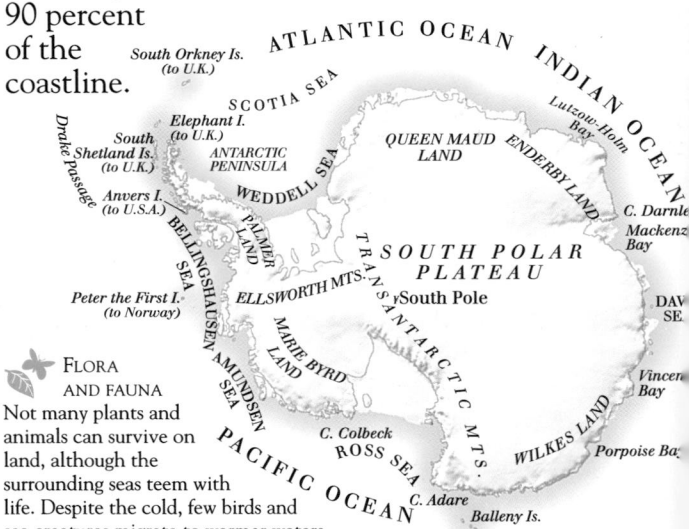

FLORA AND FAUNA

Not many plants and animals can survive on land, although the surrounding seas teem with life. Despite the cold, few birds and sea creatures migrate to warmer waters.

CLIMATE

Powerful winds form a narrow storm belt that creates severe blizzards. Summer temperatures barely reach over freezing point, and in winter the temperature can fall to –80°C (–112°F).

ENVIRONMENT

Scientists estimate that the ozone hole emerged over Antarctica in 1980. Each spring, increased sunshine activates CF(leading to rapid ozone depletion

THE ARCTIC

A FROZEN OCEAN surrounded by land, the Arctic is covered by ice up to 30 m (98 ft) thick. Most of the surrounding tundra, or vast treeless plains, are permanently frozen.

PEOPLE
The Inuit have lived in the Arctic Circle since 2500 B.C. Vikings arrived in A.D. 986.

Atlantic Ocean

Beneath the waters of the Atlantic Ocean lies the Mid-Atlantic Ridge, one of the world's longest mountain chains. Some of its peaks are so high they form islands, such as the Azores. Apart from a wide rift-valley in the centre of the ridge, the ocean consists of vast featureless plains and is 8 km (5 miles) at its deepest point.

Iceland
P 300,000
L Icelandic

Cape Verde
P 390,000
L Portuguese

ARCTIC OCEAN
GREENLAND
GREENLAND SEA
Baffin Bay
Davis Strait
Denmark Strait
ICELAND
REYKJAVIK
Faeroe Islands (to Denmark)
Murmansk
Bergen
NORTH SEA
BALTIC SEA
EUROPE
Hudson Bay
NORTH AMERICA
LABRADOR SEA
C. Farewell
Aberdeen
Rotterdam
Newfoundland
St. Lawrence
Grand Banks
New York City
Mid-Atlantic Ridge
Azores (to Portugal)
Madeira (to Portugal)
Canary Islands
Bermuda (to U.K.)
GIBRALTAR
MEDITERRANEAN SEA
BLACK SEA
Port Said

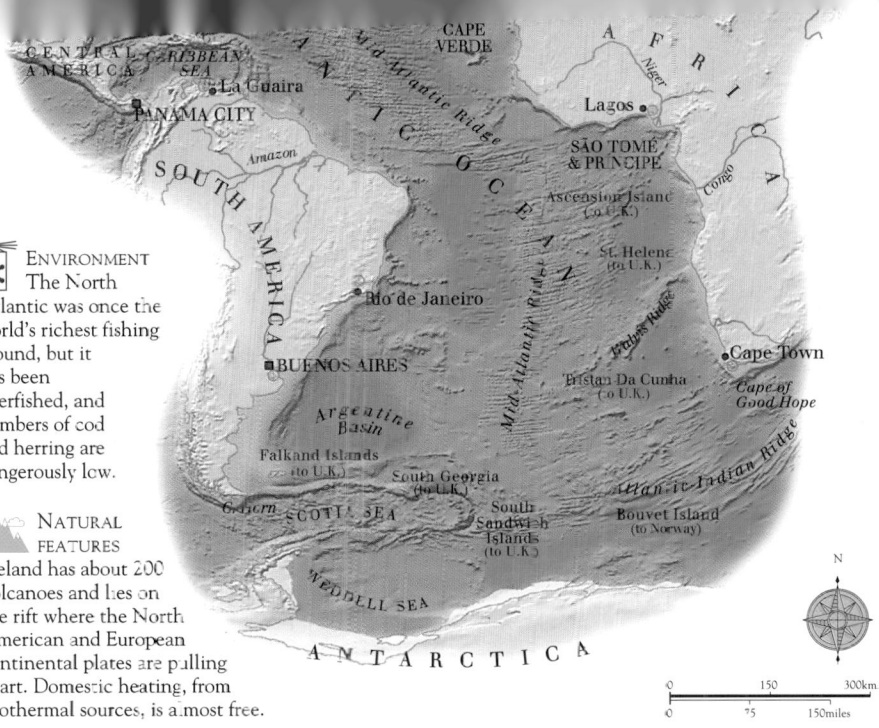

ENVIRONMENT

The North Atlantic was once the world's richest fishing ground, but it has been overfished, and numbers of cod and herring are dangerously low.

NATURAL FEATURES

Iceland has about 200 volcanoes and lies on the rift where the North American and European continental plates are pulling apart. Domestic heating, from geothermal sources, is almost free.

EUROPE

EUROPE

The Alps and the Pyrenees roughly divide the continent into north and south, forming a barrier that protects warm southern countries, such as Spain and Italy, from cold northern winds. Parts of Europe are moderated by the Gulf Stream, which circulates warm waters from the Caribbean, and even seas in the Arctic Circle stay ice-free in winter.

BARENTS SEA
FINLAND
ESTONIA
LATVIA
LITHUANIA
BELORUSSIA
RUSSIAN FEDERATION
UKRAINE
16
ROMANIA
13
BULGARIA
14
15
GREECE
BLACK SEA
GEORGIA
AZERBAIJAN
ARMENIA
1 Netherlands
2 Belgium
3 Luxembourg
4 Liechtenstein
5 Switzerland
6 Andorra
7 Monaco
8 Vatican City
9 San Marino
10 Slovenia
11 Croatia
12 Bosnia/Herzegovina
13 Yugoslavia
14 Macedonia
15 Albania
16 Moldavia

SCANDINAVIA AND FINLAND

DURING PAST ICE AGES, much of Scandinavia and Finland were covered in glaciers that carved out the land, leaving steep-sided valleys, fjords, and lakes. The Finnish, originally from the east via Russia, differ from Scandinavians in culture and language.

FINLAND
P 5 million
L Finnish, Swedish

CLIMATE
Norway's west coast is warmed by the Gulf Stream. Northern temperatures fall to –30°C (–22°F) during the six-month winter; the south is milder.

INDUSTRY
Fishing, timber, wood-pulp, paper, oil, gas, car manufacture. Norway is western Europe's largest producer of oil.

NORWAY
P 4.2 million
L Norwegian

ARCTIC OCEAN
North Cape
Hammerfest
Tromsø
Lofoten Vesterålen
NORWEGIAN SEA
L. Inari
Tana
Utsjoki
Ounas
Torne
L. Torne
Muonio
RUSSIAN FEDERATION
FINLAND
L. Uddjaur
Oulu
Oulu
Um

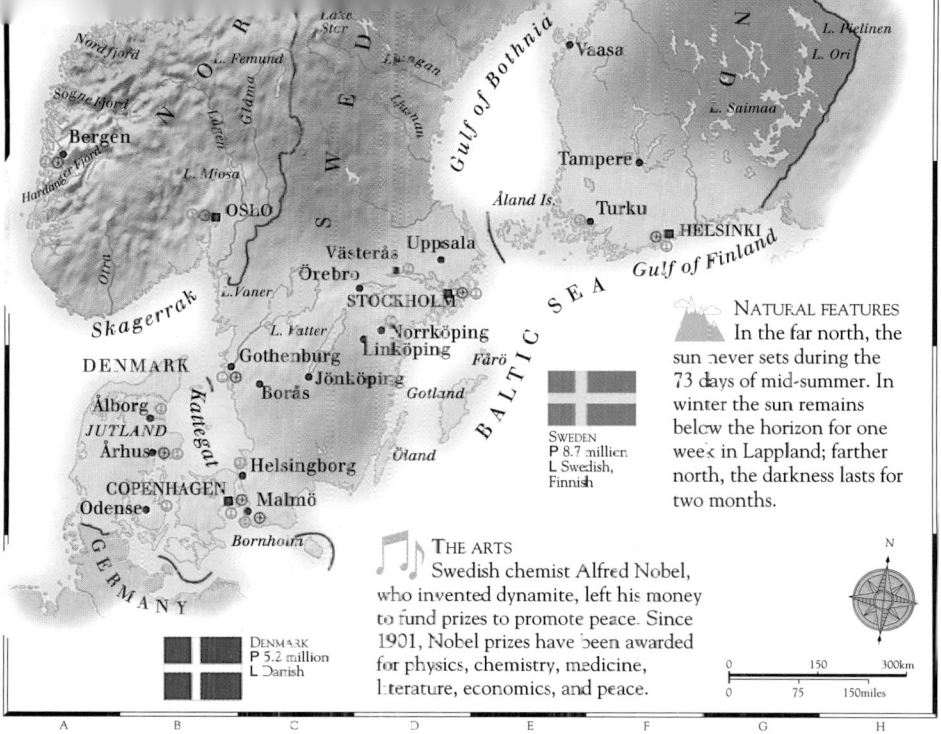

DENMARK
P 5.2 million
L Danish

SWEDEN
P 8.7 million
L Swedish, Finnish

NATURAL FEATURES

In the far north, the sun never sets during the 73 days of mid-summer. In winter the sun remains below the horizon for one week in Lappland; farther north, the darkness lasts for two months.

THE ARTS

Swedish chemist Alfred Nobel, who invented dynamite, left his money to fund prizes to promote peace. Since 1901, Nobel prizes have been awarded for physics, chemistry, medicine, literature, economics, and peace.

THE BRITISH ISLES

LYING OFF THE COAST of mainland Europe, the British Isles consist of two main islands, Ireland and Great Britain, and many smaller islands. England, Scotland, Wales, and Northern Ireland form the United Kingdom (U.K.). The Republic of Ireland became independent of the U.K. in 1921.

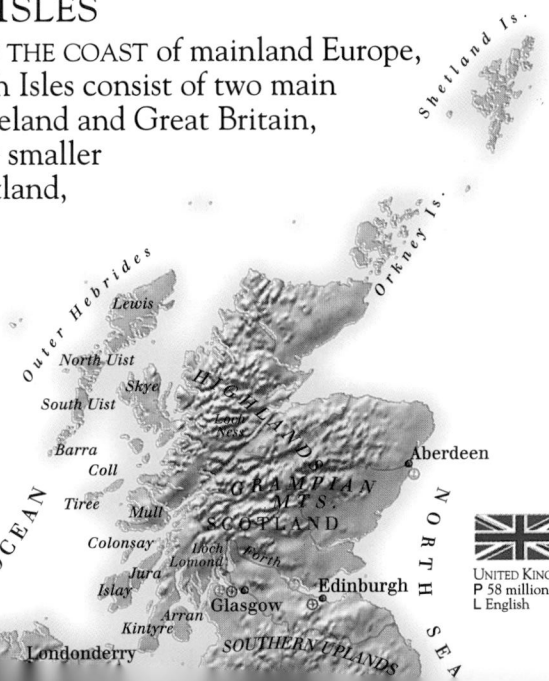

NATURAL FEATURES
The highest point in the British Isles is Ben Nevis in Scotland at a height of 1,343 m

UNITED KINGDOM
P 58 million
L English

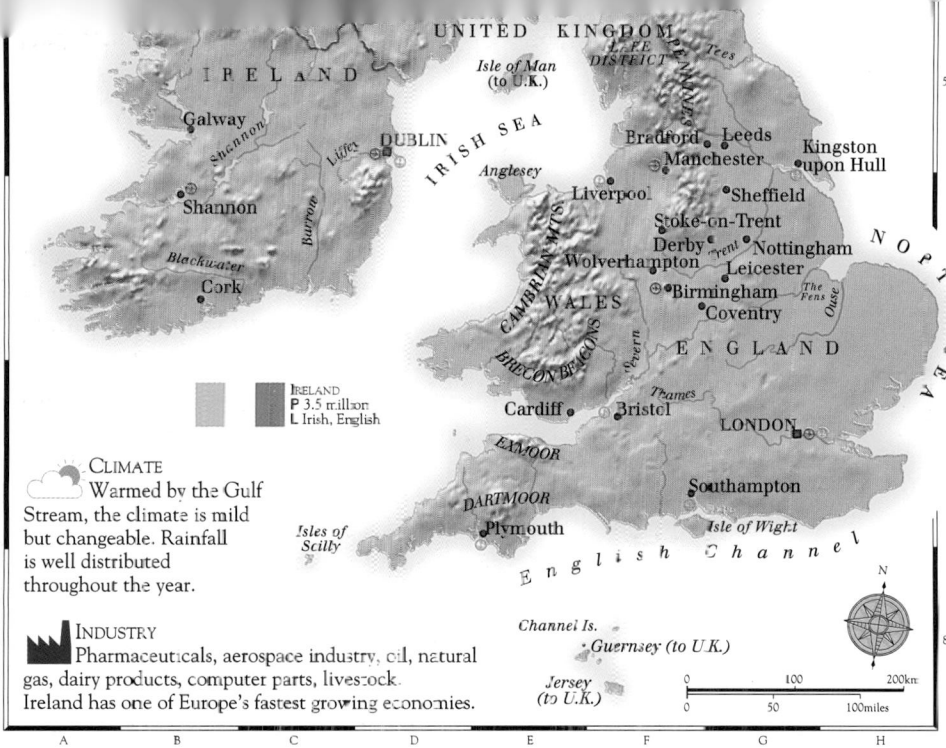

CLIMATE

Warmed by the Gulf Stream, the climate is mild but changeable. Rainfall is well distributed throughout the year.

INDUSTRY

Pharmaceuticals, aerospace industry, oil, natural gas, dairy products, computer parts, livestock. Ireland has one of Europe's fastest growing economies.

SPAIN AND PORTUGAL

SUPREME SKILL IN shipbuilding and navigation enabled both Spain and Portugal to become the most powerful empires of the 16th century. Both have a seafaring history; Christopher Columbus sailed to America in 1492, and Vasco da Gama, the Portuguese explorer, was the first to sail around Africa to India in 1497.

INDUSTRY

Fishing, car manufacture, olives, cork, ship building, citrus fruit, tourism. Spain and Portugal are famous for fortified wines. Sherry is named after Jerez de la Frontera, Spain, and Port after Porto, Portugal.

CLIMATE

Spain's coastal areas are milder than the central plateau, which has a more extreme temperature range. Almeria, Spain, contains Europe's only desert. Portugal's Mediterranean climate is moderated by the Atlantic.

PORTUGAL
P 9.9 million
L Portuguese

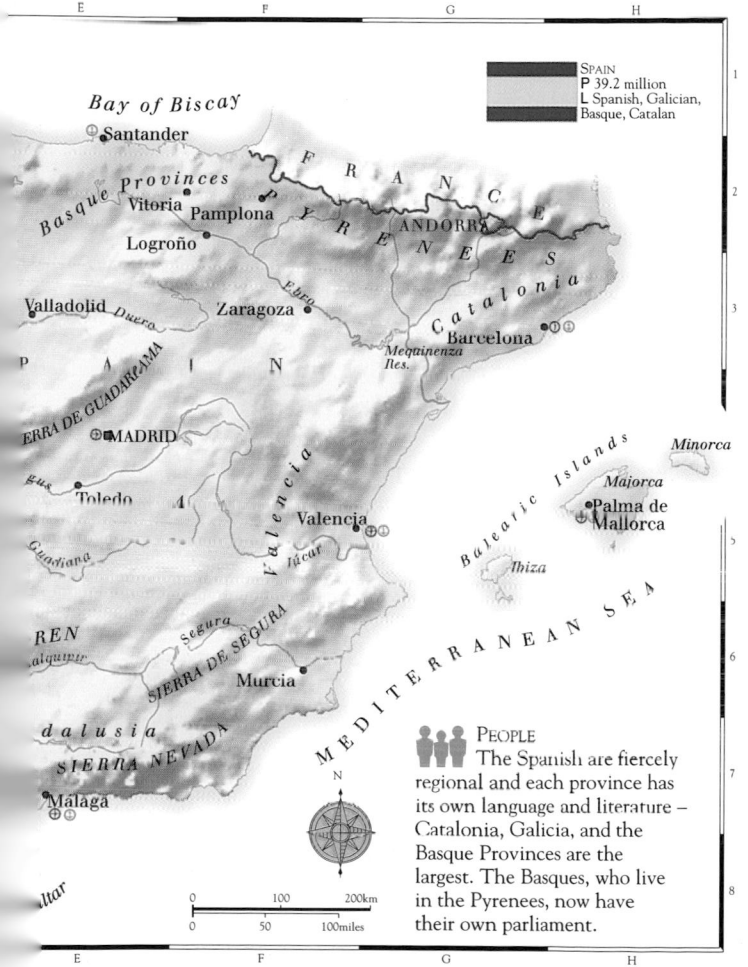

PEOPLE

The Spanish are fiercely regional and each province has its own language and literature – Catalonia, Galicia, and the Basque Provinces are the largest. The Basques, who live in the Pyrenees, now have their own parliament.

FRANCE

FOLLOWING THE FRENCH Revolution (1789–99), France became Europe's first modern republic, and possessed a colonial empire that included parts of Asia and Africa. France and Spain jointly governed Andorra from 1278. In 1993 the principality held its first full elections. The country of Monaco is a lucrative banking centre.

PEOPLE

Despite a strong national identity, the Bretons, Normans, Alsatians, Corsicans, and the Monegasque from Monaco still maintain their regional traditions.

ANDORRA
P 58,000
L Catalan

0 75 150km
0 50 100miles

COMMUNICATIONS

The French lead the world in high-speed train technology. First run in 1981, the TGV (*Train à Grande Vitesse*) is one of the world's fastest trains, with a top speed of 300 km/h (186 mph).

English Channel
Cherbourg
Le Havre
Channel Islands (to U.K.)
Caen
NORMANDY
Île d'Ouessant
Brest
BRITTANY
Rennes
Le Mans
Belle Île
Loire
Nantes
ATLANTIC OCEAN
Poitiers
Bordeaux
Garon
PYRENE
SPAI

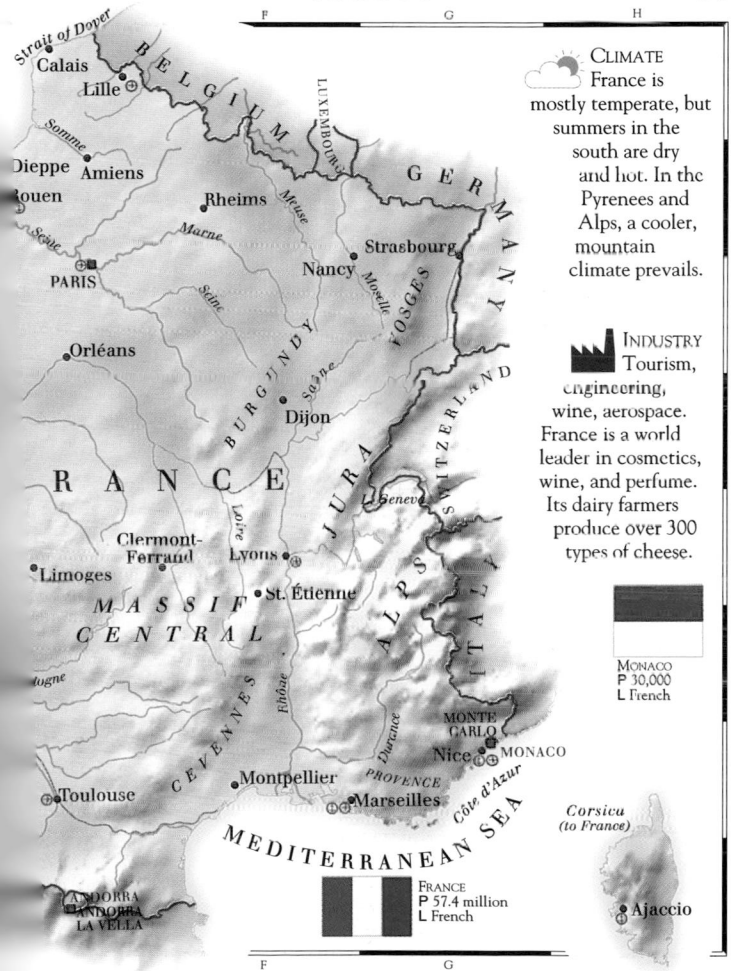
F
G
H
1
2
3
4
5
6
7
8
Strait of Dover
Calais
Lille
BELGIUM
LUXEMBOURG
GERMANY
Somme
Dieppe
Amiens
Rouen
Rheims
Meuse
Marne
Seine
PARIS
Strasbourg
Nancy
Moselle
VOSGES
Seine
Orléans
BURGUNDY
Saône
Dijon
SWITZERLAND
JURA
FRANCE
Geneva
Loire
Clermont-Ferrand
Lyons
Limoges
St. Étienne
MASSIF CENTRAL
ALPS
ITALY
Rhône
CÉVENNES
Durance
MONTE CARLO
Nice
MONACO
PROVENCE
Côte d'Azur
Montpellier
Toulouse
Marseilles
MEDITERRANEAN SEA
Corsica (to France)
Ajaccio
ANDORRA
ANDORRA LA VELLA
CLIMATE
France is mostly temperate, but summers in the south are dry and hot. In the Pyrenees and Alps, a cooler, mountain climate prevails.
INDUSTRY
Tourism, engineering, wine, aerospace. France is a world leader in cosmetics, wine, and perfume. Its dairy farmers produce over 300 types of cheese.
MONACO
P 30,000
L French
FRANCE
P 57.4 million
L French

THE LOW COUNTRIES

BELGIUM, THE NETHERLANDS, and Luxembourg are known as the "Low Countries" because they are flat and low-lying. Much of the Netherlands lies below sea level and has been reclaimed from the sea. The Low Countries, also called "Benelux", are Europe's most densely populated countries.

CLIMATE
The region is mostly temperate. Coastal areas are mildest, warmed by the Gulf Stream. Luxembourg's winters are cold

West Frisian Is.
Waddenzee
Leeuwarden
Groningen
Assen
IJsselmeer
GERMANY
IJssel
Zwolle
Flevoland
Haarlem
AMSTERDAM
NORTH SEA
ZUIDERZEE
Enschede
Apeldoorn
The Hague
Utrecht
Arnhem
Rotterdam
Dordrecht
Rhine
Nijmegen
Breda
's-Hertogenbosch
Maas

NETHERLANDS
P 15.3 million
L Dutch

BELGIUM
P 10 million
L Dutch, French, German

HISTORY
The European Union (EU) was set up in 1957 with Brussels as its administrative capital. The European Court of Justice and Investment Bank are in Luxembourg.

ENVIRONMENT
To prevent coastal areas from flooding, the Dutch built windmills to pump excess water into canals. 900 windmills encircled Amsterdam. Today, the Dutch use a giant infrastructure of canals, dykes, and dunes.

INDUSTRY
High-tech industries, cheese, flowers, metal products, banking. Many of the world's diamonds are cut, polished, and sold in Antwerp and Amsterdam. Luxembourg is a banking centre and tax haven.

COMMUNICATIONS
Belgium can be crossed within four hours by car or train. Its motorway network is so extensive and so well lit that, like the Great Wall of China, it can be seen from space.

LUXEMBOURG
P 400,000
L Letzeburgish

0 35 70km
0 20 40miles

GERMANY

IT WAS NOT UNTIL 1871 that many small independent states were united under Prussia to form Germany. After 1945, the country was divided again, into a democratic West Germany and a Soviet-dominated East Germany. Reunified in 1990, Germany is, with France, a leading member of the European Union and is currently Europe's strongest economic power.

INDUSTRY
Cars, heavy and precision engineering, electronics, chemicals. Germany has a strong industrial sector and is Europe's main car producer.

North Frisian
DENMARK
BALTIC SEA
Rügen
NORTH SEA
Helgoland Bay
East Frisian Is.
Kiel Canal
Kiel
Mecklenburg Bay
Rostock
Lübeck
Schwerin
Hamburg
L. Müritz
Bremen
Elbe
Oder
POLAND
NETHERLANDS
Ems
Dortmund - Ems Canal
SAXONY
Hanover
Brunswick
BERLIN
Potsdam
Mittelland Canal
Magdeburg
Bielefeld
Münster
Weser
HARZ
Elb
Essen
Dortmund

GERMANY
P 80.6 million
L German

CLIMATE

The Rhine Valley is mild and is suitable for wine-making. The Bavarian Alps and the Black Forest are much colder, with heavy snowfalls in winter.

HISTORY

After World War II, Berlin was shared amongst the Allies. In 1955, Berlin was divided between East and West Germany. The Berlin Wall was built in 1961 to prevent people from defecting to the West.

ENVIRONMENT

Germany has strict pollution controls, recycling most paper, glass, and used tyres. Acid rain is damaging many of Germany's forests and the Rhine is heavily polluted by industry.

0 75 150km
0 40 80miles

SWITZERLAND AND AUSTRIA

ONCE THE CENTRE OF the vast Hapsburg Empire, Austria became an independent country in 1918. Switzerland has been a neutral country since 1815, and many international organizations, such as the Red Cross, have their headquarters there. Liechtenstein is closely allied to Switzerland, which handles its foreign relations.

LIECHTENSTEIN
P 30,000
L German

SWITZERLAND
P 6.9 million
L German, French, Italian

0 50 100km
0 25 50miles

COMMUNICATIONS
The St. Gotthard road tunnel runs under the Swiss Alps. At over 16 km (10 miles) in length, it is the world's longest road tunnel.

E F G H

Climate

Altitude determines climate, with alpine areas experiencing colder temperatures and more rainfall. South of the Alps is considerably warmer and sunnier.

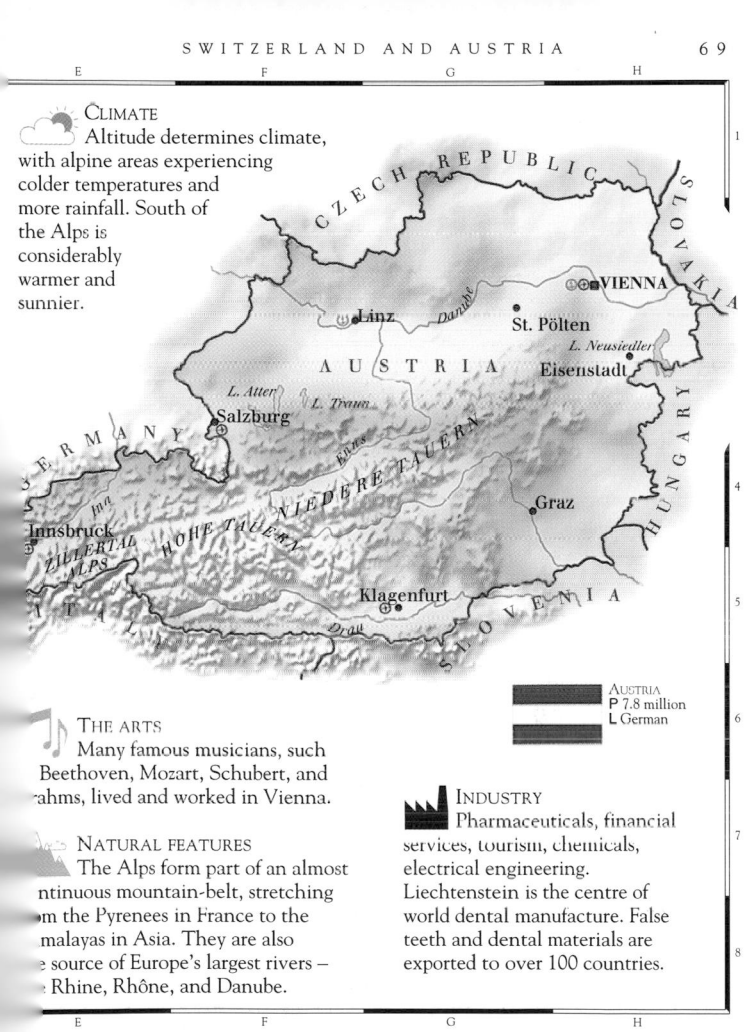

The arts

Many famous musicians, such Beethoven, Mozart, Schubert, and ahms, lived and worked in Vienna.

Natural features

The Alps form part of an almost ntinuous mountain-belt, stretching m the Pyrenees in France to the malayas in Asia. They are also e source of Europe's largest rivers – Rhine, Rhône, and Danube.

Industry

Pharmaceuticals, financial services, tourism, chemicals, electrical engineering. Liechtenstein is the centre of world dental manufacture. False teeth and dental materials are exported to over 100 countries.

E F G H

CENTRAL EUROPE

HISTORICALLY AN unstable part of the continent, central Europe became part of the Eastern Bloc after World War II. Czechoslovakia and Poland had governments with strong ties to the former U.S.S.R. In 1989, they broke away from communism, and in 1993 Czechoslovakia split into the Czech Republic and Slovakia. Poland is still moving slowly towards a market economy.

CZECH REPUBLIC
P 10.4 million
L Czech

CLIMATE
Central Europe has a continental climate, with wet springs, late summers, and cold winters. Snow can cover eastern Poland for almost three months of each year.

BALTI
Pomeranian Bay
POMERANI
Odra
Warta
Poznań
Odra
GERMANY
Wroc
SUDETEN MOUNT
Ohře
Labe
PRAGUE
(PRAHA)
Plzeň
CZECH REPUBL
Vltava
L. Vltava
BOHEMIA
MOR
Jihlava
Lužnice
AUSTRIA
BRATISLAV

POLAND
P 38.5 million
L Polish

INDUSTRY
Wood industries, coal, sulphur, iron, steel, copper, fruit. Beer, made from barley grown locally, is one of the best-known products to come out of the Czech Republic. Mining and metal production has a long history in Slovakia, and Poland is a major world exporter of coal.

ENVIRONMENT
After 1945, the central European states industrialized rapidly. Today, only four per cent of Poland's rivers have water fit for consumption, and half of its cities have no sewage treatment facilities. In central Europe acid rain has harmed trees and eroded buildings across the region.

SLOVAKIA
P 5.3 million
L Slovak

ITALY AND MALTA

THE BOOT-SHAPED PENINSULA of Italy stretches from the Alps to the Ionian Sea and includes Sardinia, Sicily, and other small, offshore islands. Italy also contains two independent enclaves – the Vatican City in Rome and the Republic of San Marino near Rimini. The Romans, Arabs, French, Turks, Spanish, and British have all fought for or colonized Malta, which has been independent since 1964.

PEOPLE
The Venetians were a seafaring people, whose ships carried silks and spices from Asia. The Venetian trader and explorer Marco Polo is said to have brought the recipe for pasta from China.

HISTORY
Italy was once a collection of small kingdoms and city-states, which were vulnerable to internal wars. It was united in 1870, through the efforts of the soldier Guiseppe Garibaldi and the politician Count Camillo di Cavour.

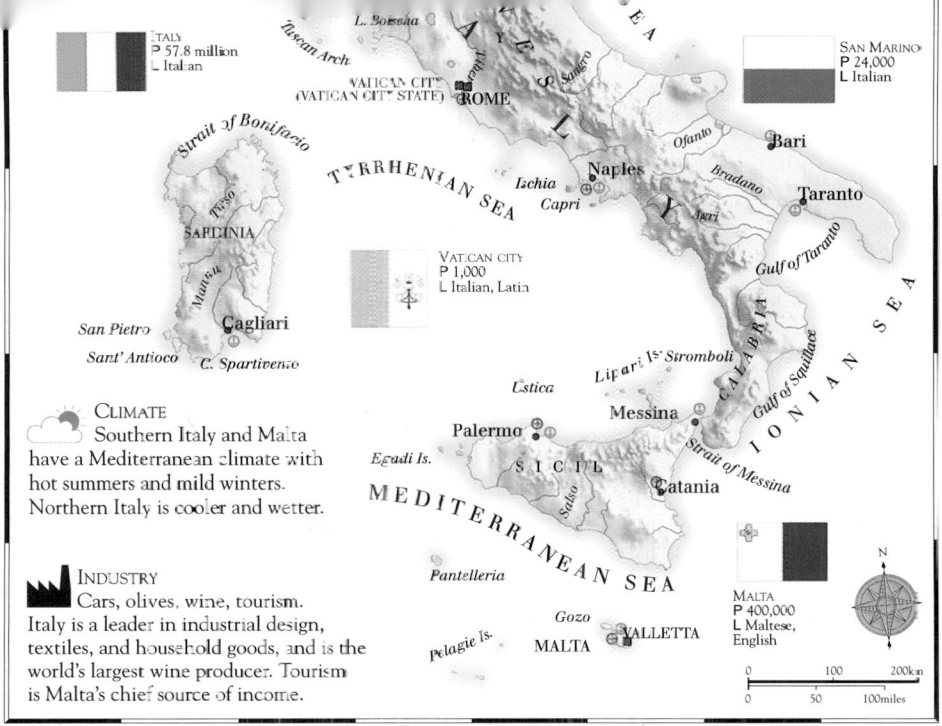

CLIMATE
Southern Italy and Malta have a Mediterranean climate with hot summers and mild winters. Northern Italy is cooler and wetter.

INDUSTRY
Cars, olives, wine, tourism. Italy is a leader in industrial design, textiles, and household goods, and is the world's largest wine producer. Tourism is Malta's chief source of income.

SOUTH CENTRAL EUROPE

FOR CENTURIES the countries of this region have had strong ties with Europe. In the early 1990s Slovenia, Croatia, and Bosnia and Herzegovina declared their independence from Yugoslavia, to which they had been annexed after World War 1. This area boasts the snow-capped Alps, the sunny Adriatic Sea in the south, as well as Hungary's fertile plain.

SLOVENIA
P 2 million
L Slovene

CROATIA
P 4.9 million
L Croatian

CLIMATE

The climate in the region is just as varied as its geography. The interior has a continental climate, with warm summers and bitterly cold winters. Coastal areas in Croatia benefit from Mediterranean temperatures suitable for growing plums, apricots, and grapes.

ITALY
AUSTRIA
Zala
Maribor
Čakovec
LJUBLJANA
Sava
SLOVENIA
ZAGREB
Česma
CR
Kupa
Prijedo
C. Kamenjak
Cres
Una
Pag
Zadar
DALM
ADRIATIC SEA
Split
C.Ploča
Brač
Hvar

N

0 75 150km
0 50 100miles

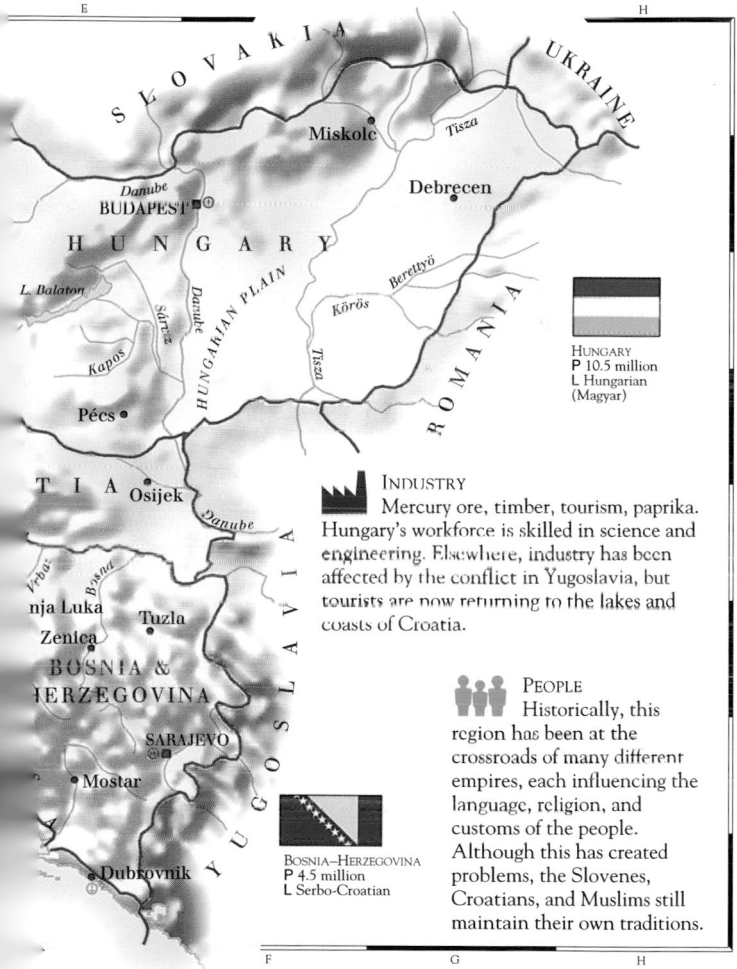

INDUSTRY

Mercury ore, timber, tourism, paprika. Hungary's workforce is skilled in science and engineering. Elsewhere, industry has been affected by the conflict in Yugoslavia, but tourists are now returning to the lakes and coasts of Croatia.

PEOPLE

Historically, this region has been at the crossroads of many different empires, each influencing the language, religion, and customs of the people. Although this has created problems, the Slovenes, Croatians, and Muslims still maintain their own traditions.

SOUTHEAST EUROPE

THIS REGION IS often referred to as the Balkans, from the Turkish word for "mountain". It is made up of countries that have a long history of invasion and occupation. From its source in the Alps, the mighty River Danube flows eastwards through Romania and Bulgaria, before pouring into the Black Sea.

YUGOSLAVIA
P 10.6 million
L Serbo-Croatian

ROMANIA
P 23.4 million
L Romanian

BULGARIA
P 8.9 million
L Bulgarian

ALBANIA
P 3.3 million
L Albanian

MACEDONIA
P 1.9 million
L Macedonian

History

Over the past decade all the countries in this region have gained independence from the Russian communist bloc. This led to the breakup of the former Yugoslavia in 1991. When the states of Serbia and Montenegro combined to form the new Federal Republic of Yugoslavia, it resulted in a war which lasted from 1991–95.

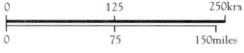

Climate

Hot or cold winds from Russia can bring spells of extreme weather in Romania and Bulgaria. Snow may even stay on the peaks until mid-summer. Yugoslavia and Macedonia have warm summers that are good for growing early fruit crops.

Industry

Coal, wine, tobacco, iron ore, tourism. Black Sea tourism is being developed in Romania to generate income to help improve the lives of the people. In the foothills of the Balkan Mountains in Bulgaria most of the world's rose oil is produced.

GREECE

SURROUNDED BY THE Aegean, Ionian, and Cretan seas, no part of Greece is more than 137 km (85 miles) from the coast. Its territory includes the mainland on the Balkan peninsula, and more than 1,400 islands. The country is mountainous and less than one-third of the land is cultivated. Greece gained its independence in 1830 after a long and fierce war, ending 400 years of Turkish rule.

CLIMATE

Northwestern Greece is alpine, while parts of Crete are almost subtropical. The islands and the large central plain of the mainland have a Mediterranean climate, with high summer temperatures and mild winters.

GREECE
P 10.2 million
L Greek

ENVIRONMENT

Athens suffers from smog, known as *nefos*, which damages its ancient monuments. The Parthenon, part of the Acropolis, has suffered more erosion in the previous two decades than in the past two thousand years.

HISTORY

Regarded as the founders of democracy, the ancient Greeks were advanced for their time. They were the first to study medicine, geometry, and physics (on a scientific basis), and Greece was home to great thinkers such as Plato, Aristotle, and Socrates.

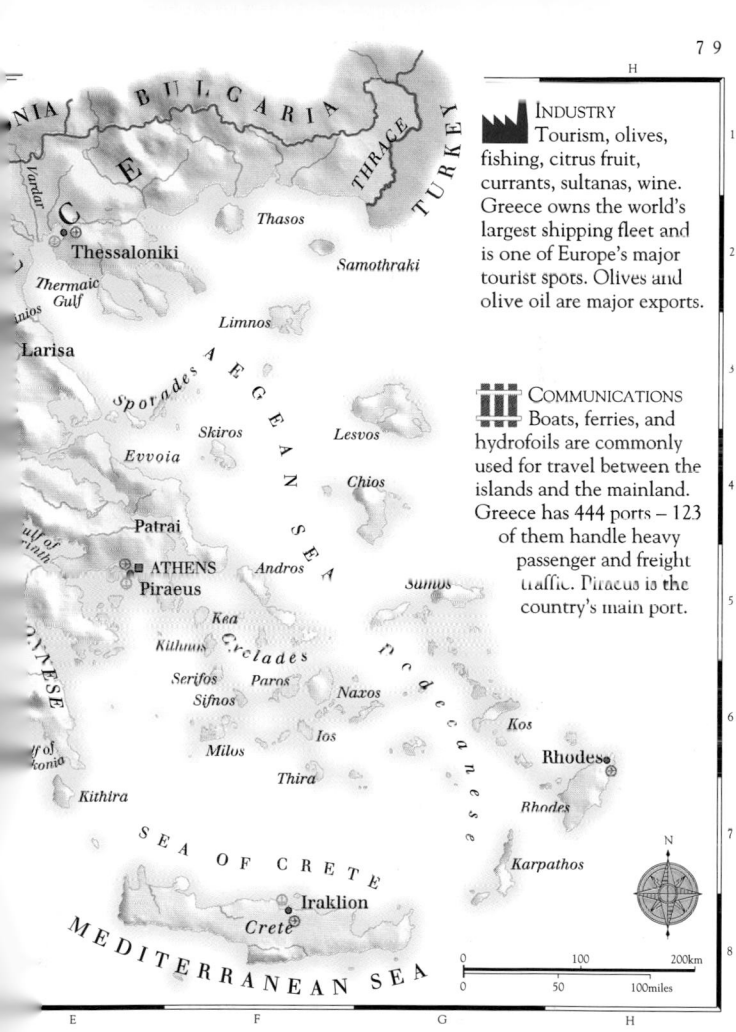

INDUSTRY
Tourism, olives, fishing, citrus fruit, currants, sultanas, wine. Greece owns the world's largest shipping fleet and is one of Europe's major tourist spots. Olives and olive oil are major exports.

COMMUNICATIONS
Boats, ferries, and hydrofoils are commonly used for travel between the islands and the mainland. Greece has 444 ports – 123 of them handle heavy passenger and freight traffic. Piraeus is the country's main port.

THE BALTIC STATES AND BELORUSSIA

LITHUANIA, ESTONIA, AND LATVIA – the three Baltic States – were the first republics to declare independence from the Soviet Union in 1990-91. There is now tension between native Estonians and Russians, who make up a third of the population. Belorussia's capital, Minsk, is the headquarters of the organization that brings together former Soviet States – the Confederation of Independent States (CIS).

PEOPLE
Russians, Belorussians, and Ukrainians resettled in Latvia when it was part of the U.S.S.R. Today Latvians make up only about half of the whole population, and they are a minority in the capital.

LITHUANIA
P 3.8 million

ESTONIA
P 1.6 million
L Estonian

LATVIA
P 2.7 million
L Latvian

BELORUSSIA
P 10.3 million
L Belorussian

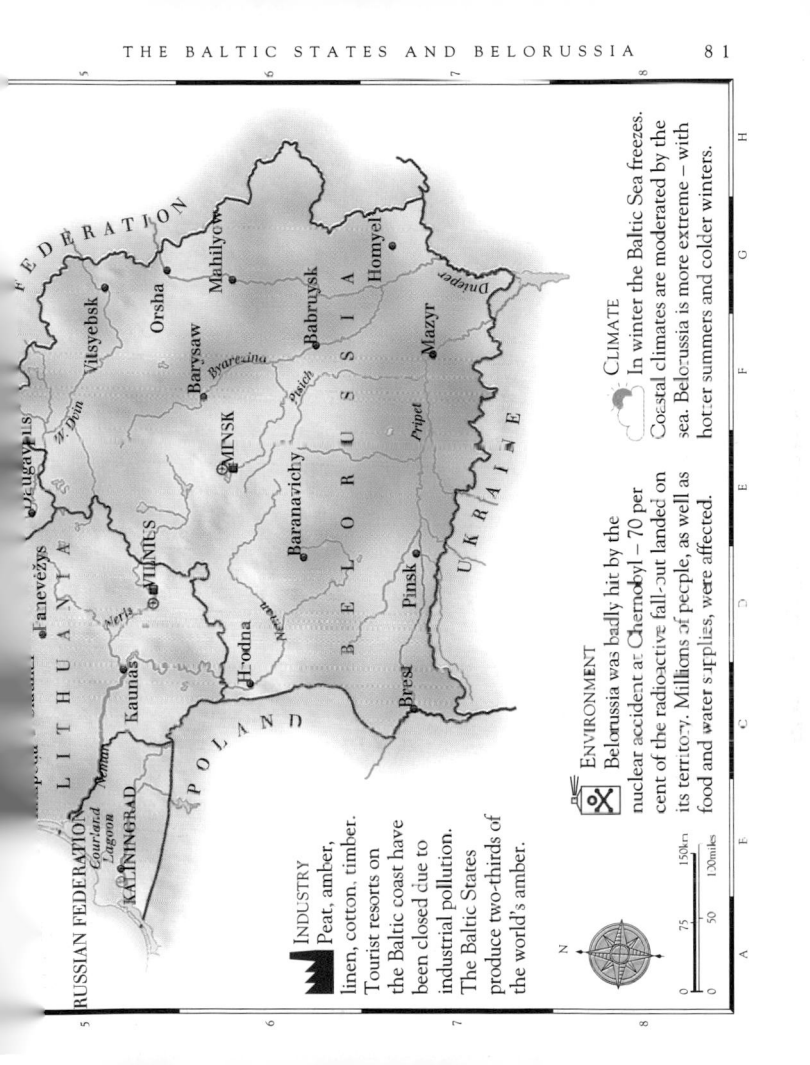
RUSSIAN FEDERATION
KALININGRAD
Courland Lagoon
Neman
LITHUANIA
Kaunas
Nerta
VILNIUS
Panevėžys
Daugavpils
W. Dvina
Vitsyebsk
POLAND
Hrodna
Nemen
Orsha
Mahilyow
Barysaw
Byarezina
MINSK
Baranavichy
Pasich
Babruysk
BELORUSSIA
Homyel
Pripet
Pinsk
Brest
Mazyr
Dnieper
UKRAINE
FEDERATION
INDUSTRY
Peat, amber, linen, cotton, timber. Tourist resorts on the Baltic coast have been closed due to industrial pollution. The Baltic States produce two-thirds of the world's amber.
ENVIRONMENT
Belorussia was badly hit by the nuclear accident at Chernobyl – 70 per cent of the radioactive fall-out landed on its territory. Millions of people, as well as food and water supplies, were affected.
CLIMATE
In winter the Baltic Sea freezes. Coastal climates are moderated by the sea. Belorussia is more extreme – with hotter summers and colder winters.
N
0 75 150km
0 50 120miles
A B C D E F G H
5 6 7 8

EUROPEAN RUSSIA

SPANNING THE TWO continents of Europe and Asia, the Russian Federation is the world's largest country. In 1917, the world's first communist government took power and in 1923, Russia became the U.S.S.R., which included many territories that were once part of the Russian Empire. Economic reforms in the 1980s led to changes resulting in the fall of communism in 1991.

INDUSTRY
Oil, gas, gold, diamonds, hydrocarbons, precious metals. Russia has large reserves of iron, coal, and nickel. Huge factories, which have grown without environmental controls, are causing pollution problems.

HISTORY

Some believe that Russia took its name from a Viking tribe called *Varangian Russes*. The first Russian state was established at Kiev in A.D 800.

CLIMATE

Russia has a cold continental climate, open to influence by the Arctic and Atlantic Oceans. Snow covers more than half the country for six months of the year.

COMMUNICATIONS

The Trans–Siberian Railway, started in 1881 and completed in 1916, is the longest continuous rail line in the world. The 9,310 km (5,785 mile) journey from Moscow to Vladivostok takes seven days.

THE ARTS

The Hermitage Museum in St. Petersburg contains 2.5 million objects in 1,000 rooms. Its buildings include the Winter Palace, which was stormed in the 1917 Revolution by Lenin's Bolshevik forces.

UKRAINE AND THE CAUCASUS

SEPARATED FROM the Russian Federation by the Caucasus mountains, the newly independent Caucasian Republics – Armenia, Azerbaijan, and Georgia – are rich in natural resources. The Ukraine, Europe's largest country, is dominated by a flat and fertile plain.

ENVIRONMENT
As a result of the 1986 Chernobyl nuclear disaster, 4 million Ukrainians live in radioactive areas. In 1994, reactors from the Chernobyl plant were still being used to provide nuclear power.

MOLDAVIA
P 4.4 million
L Romanian

CLIMATE
Ukraine and Moldavia have a continental climate, with distinctive seasons. Armenia, Azerbaijan, and Georgia are protected from cold air from the north by the Caucasus mountains.

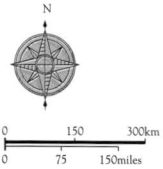

INDUSTRY
Coal, iron, cars, wine, citrus fruit, cotton, minerals. The Ukraine was known as the "breadbasket" of the Soviet Union as its steppes were extensively cultivated. Georgia's known oil reserve are as yet unexploited.

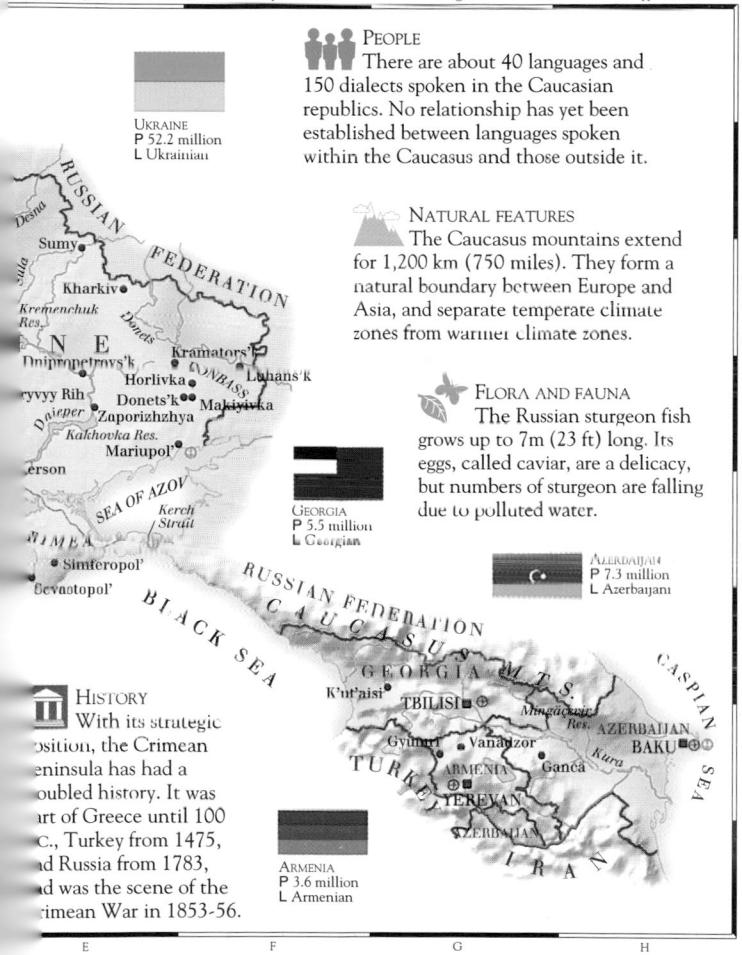

UKRAINE
P 52.2 million
L Ukrainian

GEORGIA
P 5.5 million
L Georgian

AZERBAIJAN
P 7.3 million
L Azerbaijani

ARMENIA
P 3.6 million
L Armenian

PEOPLE

There are about 40 languages and 150 dialects spoken in the Caucasian republics. No relationship has yet been established between languages spoken within the Caucasus and those outside it.

NATURAL FEATURES

The Caucasus mountains extend for 1,200 km (750 miles). They form a natural boundary between Europe and Asia, and separate temperate climate zones from warmer climate zones.

FLORA AND FAUNA

The Russian sturgeon fish grows up to 7m (23 ft) long. Its eggs, called caviar, are a delicacy, but numbers of sturgeon are falling due to polluted water.

HISTORY

With its strategic position, the Crimean peninsula has had a troubled history. It was part of Greece until 100 B.C., Turkey from 1475, and Russia from 1783, and was the scene of the Crimean War in 1853-56.

AFRICA
MEDITERRANEAN SEA
RED SEA
TUNISIA
ALGERIA
LIBYA
EGYPT
MOROCCO
WESTERN SAHARA
MAURITANIA
MALI
NIGER
CHAD
SUDAN
ERITREA
DJIBOUTI
ETHIOPIA
NIGERIA
CENTRAL AFRICAN
BURKINA
GHANA
TOGO
BENIN
IVORY COAST
GUINEA
SIERRA LEONE
GUINEA-BISSAU
GAMBIA
SENEGAL
Madeira (to Portugal)
Canary Islands (to Spain)

AFRICA

Both tropics and the equator run through Africa, the warmest of all the continents. The land around the tropics is starved of rain creating great deserts such as the Sahara and the Kalahari. In contrast, high rainfall around the equator has produced lush tropical rainforests.

NORTHWEST AFRICA

SPANNING THE continent of Africa, from the Atlantic to the Red Sea, the Sahara covers 9 million sq km (3.5 million sq miles) and is the world's largest desert. Droughts and the over-use of land for farming are causing the Sahara to spread into the Sahel (semi-arid grasslands). Italy, the U.K., Spain, and France have all had colonies in this region.

Strait of Gibraltar
Ceuta (to Spain)
Melilla (to Spain)
Tangier
RABAT
Casablanca
Fez
MOROCCO
Marrakesh
Agadir
Béchar
ATLANTIC OCEAN
ATLAS MTS.
EL AAIUN
Dakhla
WESTERN SAHARA
MAURITANIA
Morocco occupied the whole of Western Sahara in 1979.

INDUSTRY
Oil, gas, phosphates, tourism, olives, dates, fruit. Morocco and Tunisia attract millions of tourists every year. They are also leading phosphate producers. Algeria and Libya have significant oil reserves.

MOROCCO
P 27 million
L Arabic

CLIMATE
Coastal areas have a temperate climate with hot, dry summers and wet winters. Mountain areas are cooler. Most areas are affected by the many different kinds of Sahara wind, such as the *sirocco*, the *chergui*, and the *chili*.

NATURAL FEATURES
The Atlas Mountains exten over 2,410 km (1,500 miles) from the Canary Islands in the Atlantic to Tunisia. Like the Alps, the Atla Mountains were formed when the continental plates of Europe and Africa pushed together.

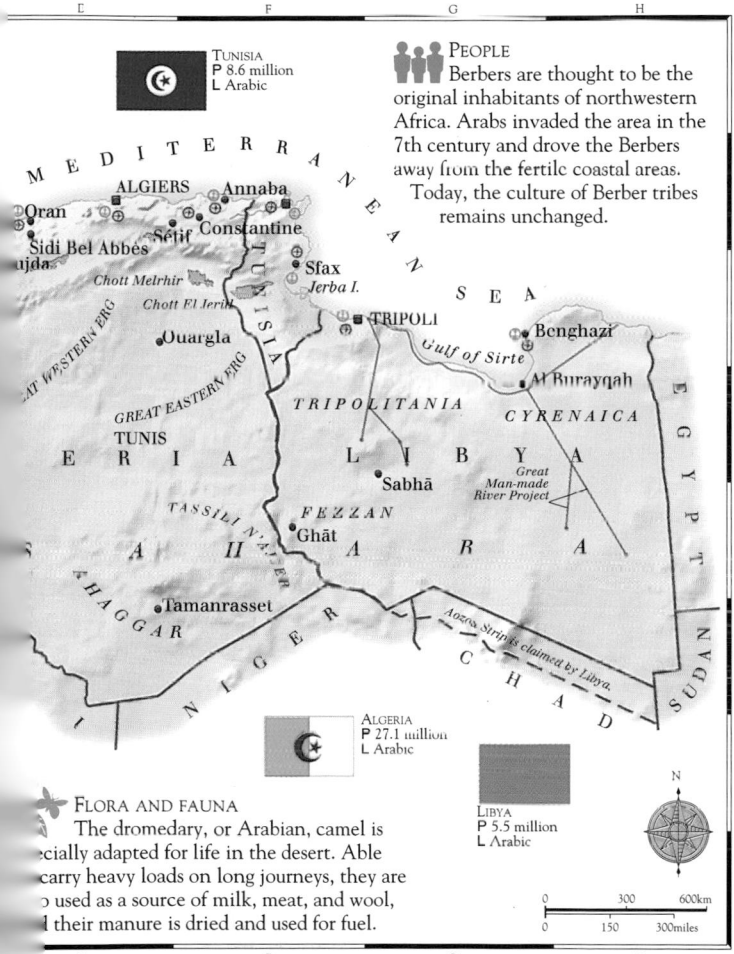

FLORA AND FAUNA

The dromedary, or Arabian, camel is specially adapted for life in the desert. Able to carry heavy loads on long journeys, they are also used as a source of milk, meat, and wool, and their manure is dried and used for fuel.

NORTHEAST AFRICA

THE NILE, THE LONGEST river in the world, carries rich mud from the highlands of Sudan into Egypt, creating some of the most fertile land in the world. About 99 per cent of Egypt's population live on the river's banks. Ethiopia, Somalia, and Sudan have been beset by drought, famine, and war and about half of Africa's 4.5 million refugees come from this area.

EGYPT
P 56.1 million
L Arabic

HISTORY

Hieroglyphs were a set of mysterious symbols until the discovery of the Rosetta Stone in 1799. The Stone is inscribed in three different scripts: ancient Greek, demotic, and hieroglyphs. By comparing the royal names in the scripts, hieroglyphs were finally deciphered 25 years later.

ERITREA
P 3.5 million
L Tigrinya, Arabic

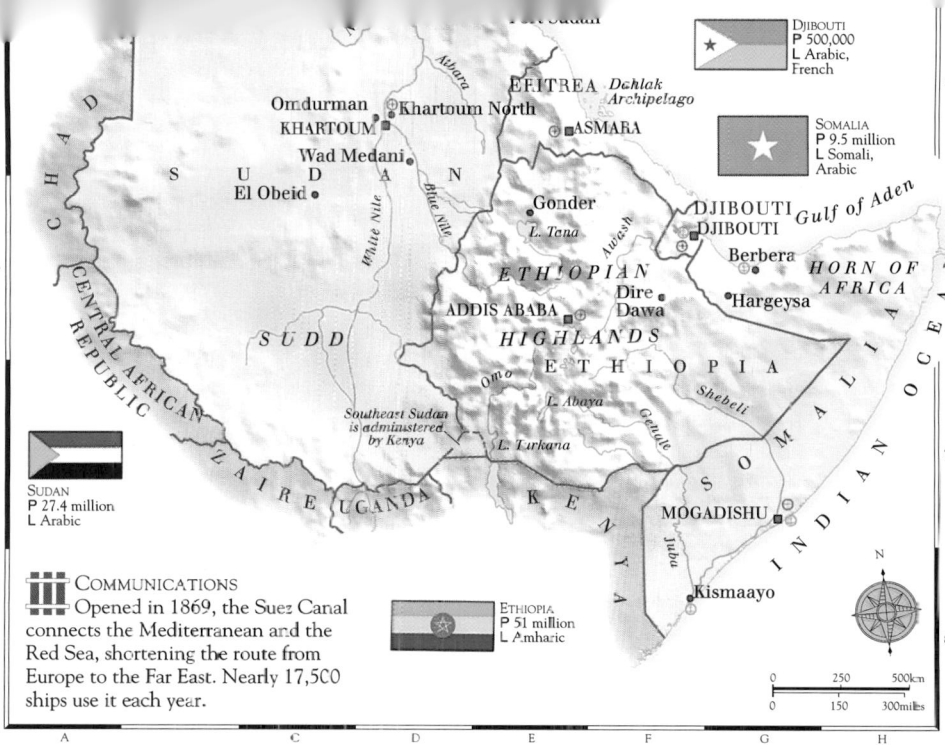

COMMUNICATIONS

Opened in 1869, the Suez Canal connects the Mediterranean and the Red Sea, shortening the route from Europe to the Far East. Nearly 17,500 ships use it each year.

WEST AFRICA

BY 1914, MANY European countries, such as France, Britain, and Portugal, had divided up most of Africa between them. Despite independence, foreign companies still own many of the coffee and cocoa plantations in the region.

GAMBIA
P 900,000
L English

INDUSTRY
Bauxite, oil, gypsum, cocoa, phosphates, peanuts, fishing. This region produces nearly half of the world's supply of cocoa beans. The world's largest deposits of gypsum are found in Mauritania.

CLIMATE
Coastal areas have a tropical climate, with high temperatures and one or two rainy seasons. The hot and dry Sahel is marked by the dusty *harmattan* wind.

GUINEA
P 6.3 million
L French

GUINEA-BISSAU
P 1 million
L Portuguese

SIERRA LEONE
P 4.5 million
L English

WESTERN SAHARA
C. Blanc
C. Timiris
MAURITANIA
NOUAKCHOTT
L. Rkiz
Senegal
SENEGAL
DAKAR
BANJUL
GAMBIA
BISSAU
GUINEA-BISSAU
Bijagós Archipelago
CONAKRY
FREETOWN
SIERRA LEONE
MONROVIA
LIBERIA
YAMOUSSOUKRO
BAMAKO
Niger
GUINEA
ATLANTIC OCEAN
Ivo

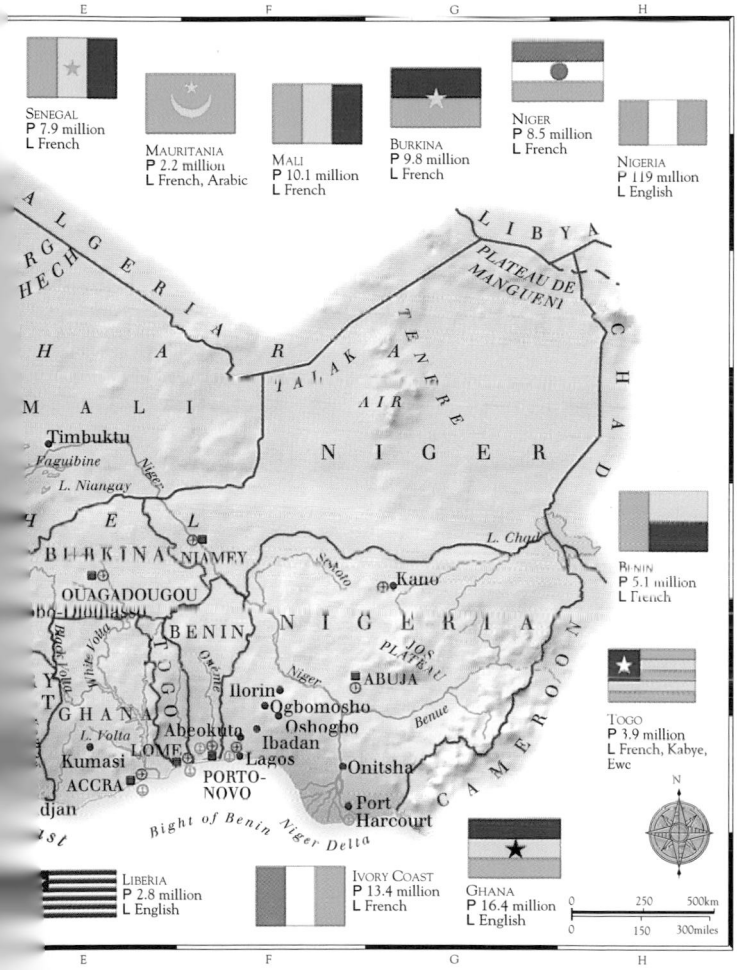
E F G H
1 2 3 4 5 6 7 8
SENEGAL
P 7.9 million
L French
MAURITANIA
P 2.2 million
L French, Arabic
MALI
P 10.1 million
L French
BURKINA
P 9.8 million
L French
NIGER
P 8.5 million
L French
NIGERIA
P 119 million
L English
ALGERIA
LIBYA
PLATEAU DE MANGUENI
TALAK
TENERE
AIR
CHAD
MALI
Timbuktu
Faguibine
L. Niangay
Niger
NIGER
NIAMEY
BURKINA
OUAGADOUGOU
L. Chad
Sokoto
Kano
BENIN
NIGERIA
JOS PLATEAU
ABUJA
White Volta
Black Volta
Owene
Niger
Benue
Ilorin
Ogbomosho
Oshogbo
Ibadan
Abeokuta
Lagos
Onitsha
Port Harcourt
GHANA
L. Volta
Kumasi
ACCRA
LOME
PORTO-NOVO
CAMEROON
Bight of Benin
Niger Delta
BENIN
P 5.1 million
L French
TOGO
P 3.9 million
L French, Kabye, Ewe
N
LIBERIA
P 2.8 million
L English
IVORY COAST
P 13.4 million
L French
GHANA
P 16.4 million
L English
0 250 500km
0 150 300miles

CENTRAL AFRICA

MUCH OF THIS region is covered in dense tropical rainforest, drained by the Congo (Zaire) River, which forms a huge arc on its way to the Atlantic. In the 16th century Portugal and Spain set up trading posts on the west coast as part of the slave trade. Millions of Africans from this region were sent as slaves to the New World. Many people in coastal areas still speak Spanish and Portuguese.

CHAD
P 6 million
L French

INDUSTRY
Timber, oil, iron, cocoa, coffee, copper. Bélinga, Gabon, contains the world's largest iron ore deposits. Many central African countries have unexploited oil and gas reserves.

CAMEROON
P 12.5 million
L French, English

EQUATORIAL GUINEA
P 400,000
L Spanish

CENTRAL AFRICAN REPUBLIC
P 3.3 million
L French

LIBYA
Aozou Strip, claimed by Libya
TIBESTI
NIGER
CHAD
L. Chad
Kousseri
N'DJAMENA
Erguig
Salamat
Maroua
Logone
Chari
Garoua
Sarh
Moundou
SUDAN
NIGERIA

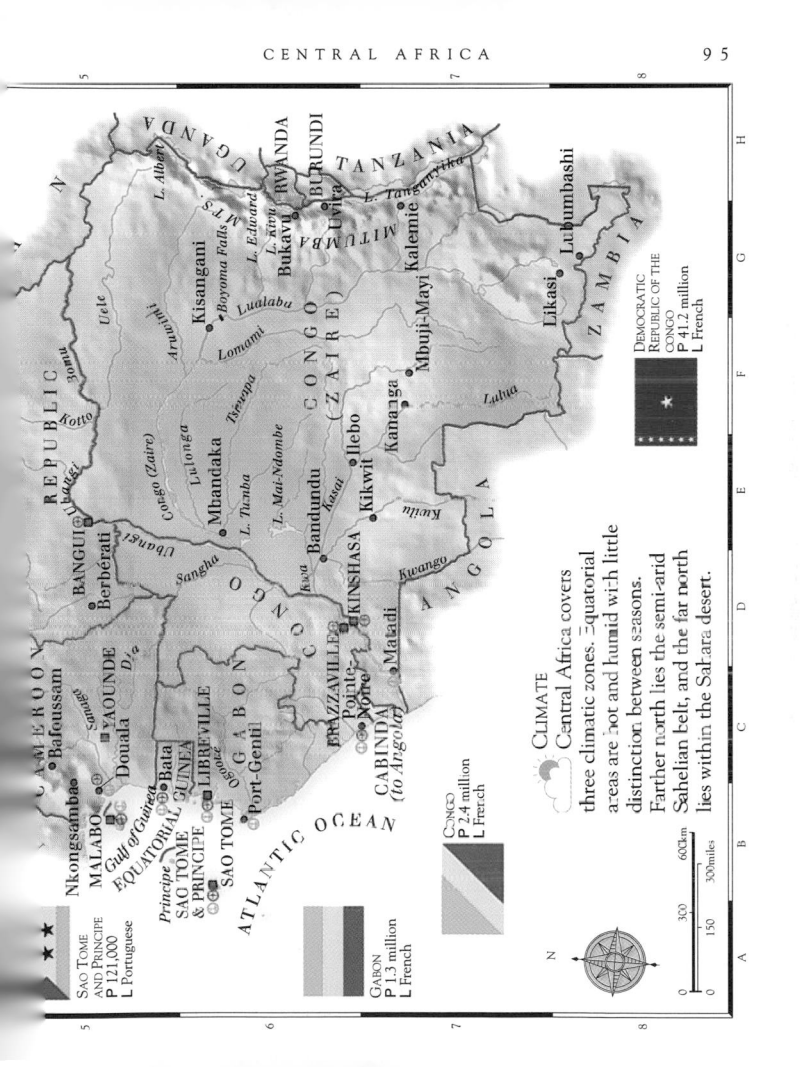
CAMEROON
Bafoussam
Nkongsamba
MALABO
YAOUNDE
Douala
Gulf of Guinea
EQUATORIAL GUINEA
Bata
Principe
SAO TOME & PRINCIPE
SAO TOME
LIBREVILLE
Port-Gentil
GABON
Berbérati
BANGUI
CENTRAL AFRICAN REPUBLIC
Kotto
Ubangi
Uele
Ubangi
Sangha
Congo (Zaire)
Mbandaka
L. Tumba
L. Mai-Ndombe
Kasai
Bandundu
Kwa
Lulonga
Tshuapa
Lomami
Arwimi
Kisangani
Boyoma Falls
Lualaba
L. Albert
UGANDA
MTS. MITUMBA
L. Edward
L. Kivu
Bukavu
RWANDA
BURUNDI
Uvira
L. Tanganyika
TANZANIA
Kalemie
Mbuji-Mayi
Kananga
Ilebo
Kikwit
Kwilu
Kwango
Luba
CONGO (ZAIRE)
KINSHASA
Matadi
Pointe Noire
BRAZZAVILLE
CABINDA (to Angola)
ANGOLA
Likasi
Lubumbashi
ZAMBIA
ATLANTIC OCEAN
SAO TOME AND PRINCIPE
P 121,000
L Portuguese
GABON
P 1.3 million
L French
CONGO
P 2.4 million
L French
CLIMATE
Central Africa covers three climatic zones. Equatorial areas are hot and humid with little distinction between seasons. Farther north lies the semi-arid Sahelian belt, and the far north lies within the Sahara desert.
N
0 300 600km
0 150 300miles
DEMOCRATIC REPUBLIC OF THE CONGO
P 41.2 million
L French
A B C D E F G H
5 6 7 8

CENTRAL EAST AFRICA

LARGE AREAS OF savannah, or grassland, in central Africa provide grazing for both domestic and wild animals. Industry is poorly developed in the region – Zambia, Rwanda, Burundi, and Uganda suffer from having no sea ports. Lake Victoria is the largest lake in Africa, and a source of the River Nile.

UGANDA
P 19.2 million
L English

KENYA
P 26.1 million
L Swahili

FLORA AND FAUNA
Poaching remains a major problem in this area. To combat this, all the countries in this region have set up wildlife parks to protect animals such as elephants and zebra.

RWANDA
P 7.5 million
L French, Kinyarwanda

INDUSTRY
Tobacco, coffee, tea, tourism, cloves, copper. Zambia is the world's fifth-largest producer of copper. Wildlife parks in this region

SUDAN
ETHIOPIA
Southeast Sudan is administered by Kenya
L. Turkana
CHALBI DESERT
SOMALIA
Albert Nile
Victoria Nile
L. Albert
L. Kyoga
UGANDA
KAMPALA
KENYA
Great Rift Valley
ABERDARE RANGE
Tana
L. Edward
Lake Victoria
NAIROBI
KIGALI
RWANDA
Mwanza
BUJUMBURA
L. Eyasi
L. Manyara
Galana
Mombasa
INDIAN OCEAN

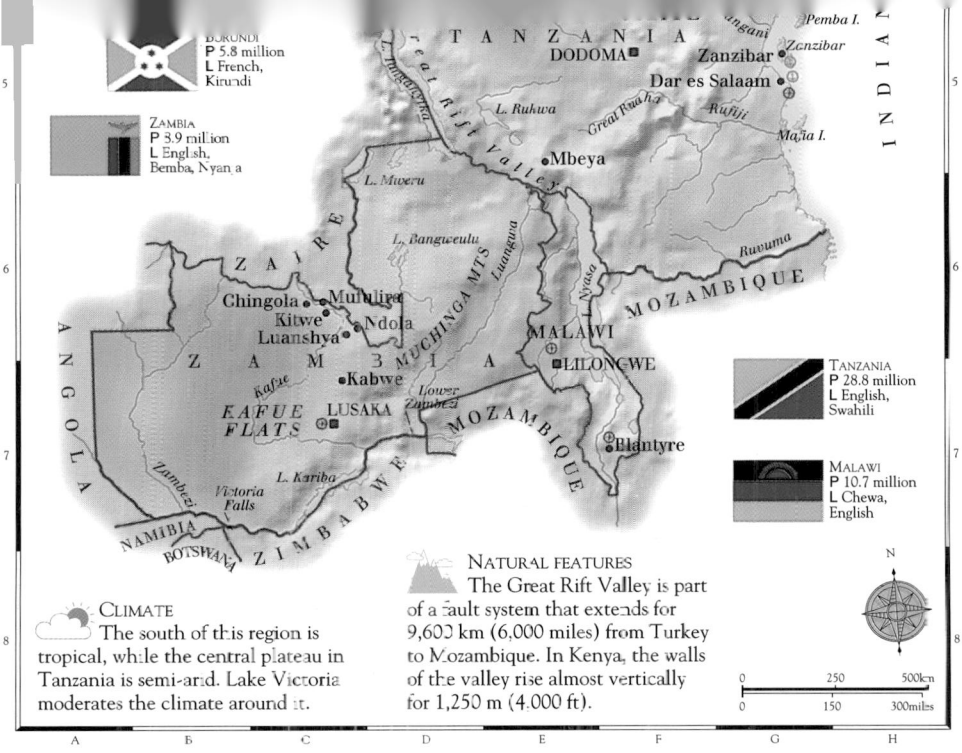

CLIMATE

The south of this region is tropical, while the central plateau in Tanzania is semi-arid. Lake Victoria moderates the climate around it.

NATURAL FEATURES

The Great Rift Valley is part of a fault system that extends for 9,600 km (6,000 miles) from Turkey to Mozambique. In Kenya, the walls of the valley rise almost vertically for 1,250 m (4,000 ft).

SOUTHERN AFRICA

SOUTHERN AFRICA'S RICH mineral resources, such as gold and diamonds, provide most of the wealth in this region, but South Africa dominates politics, work, and trade. All eight countries are independent, multi-racial democracies. South Africa had its first free elections in 1994 when Nelson Mandela was voted the country's first black president. Namibia won independence in 1990, but Angola is still torn apart by civil war.

ANGOLA
P 10.3 million
L Portuguese

ZIMBABWE
P 10.9 million
L English

MOZAMBIQUE
P 15.3 million
L Portuguese

BOTSWANA
P 1.4 million
L English

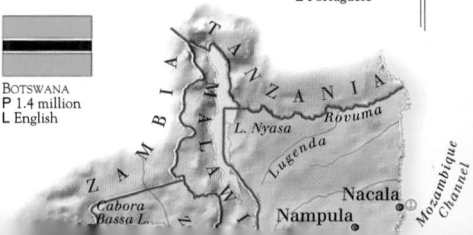

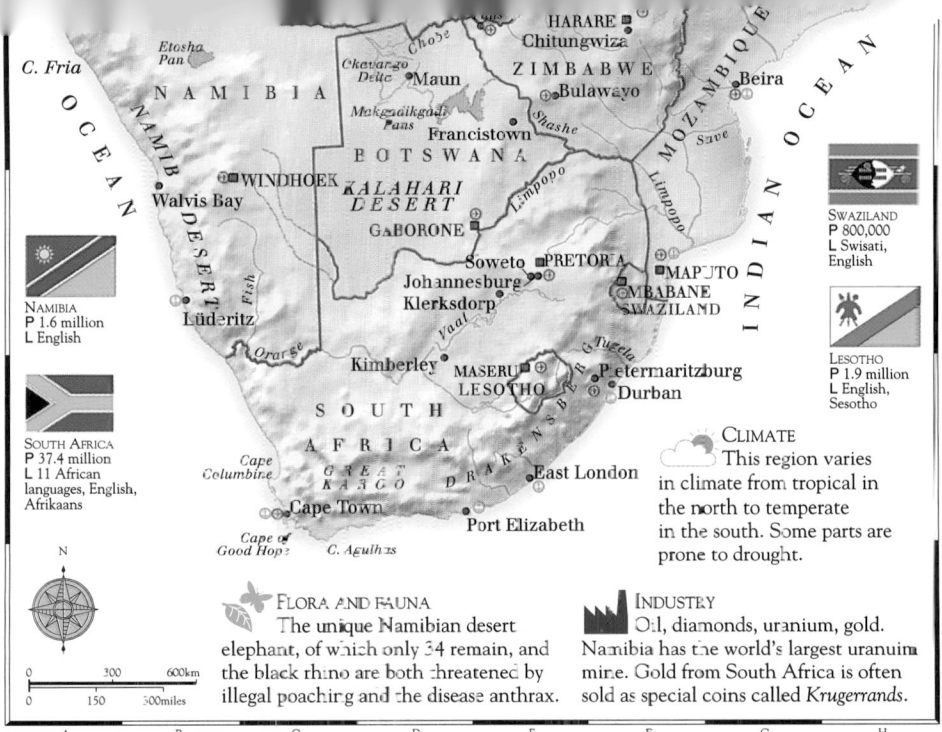

NAMIBIA
P 1.6 million
L English

SOUTH AFRICA
P 37.4 million
L 11 African languages, English, Afrikaans

SWAZILAND
P 800,000
L Swisati, English

LESOTHO
P 1.9 million
L English, Sesotho

CLIMATE
This region varies in climate from tropical in the north to temperate in the south. Some parts are prone to drought.

FLORA AND FAUNA
The unique Namibian desert elephant, of which only 34 remain, and the black rhino are both threatened by illegal poaching and the disease anthrax.

INDUSTRY
Oil, diamonds, uranium, gold. Namibia has the world's largest uranium mine. Gold from South Africa is often sold as special coins called *Krugerrands*.

Indian Ocean

The smallest of the world's oceans, the Indian Ocean has some 5,000 islands scattered across its area. Beneath its surface, three great mountain ranges converge towards the ocean's centre – an area of strong seismic and volcanic activity. The ocean's greatest depth, 7,440 m (24,400 ft), is in the Java Trench.

Flora and fauna

Owing to its position off the African coast, Madagascar is home to many unique animals, such as tenrecs, lemurs, and fossas.

Environment

The Indian Ocean is at risk from oil pollution from tankers carrying oil from the Persian Gulf.

Climate

The monsoon winds blow over the Indian Ocean – from the southwest or from the northeast according to the season. The southwesterly monsoon brings heavy rains to southern Asia.

Maldives
P 13.3 million
L Divehi

Seychelles
P 69,000

Comoros
P 497,000
L Arabic, French

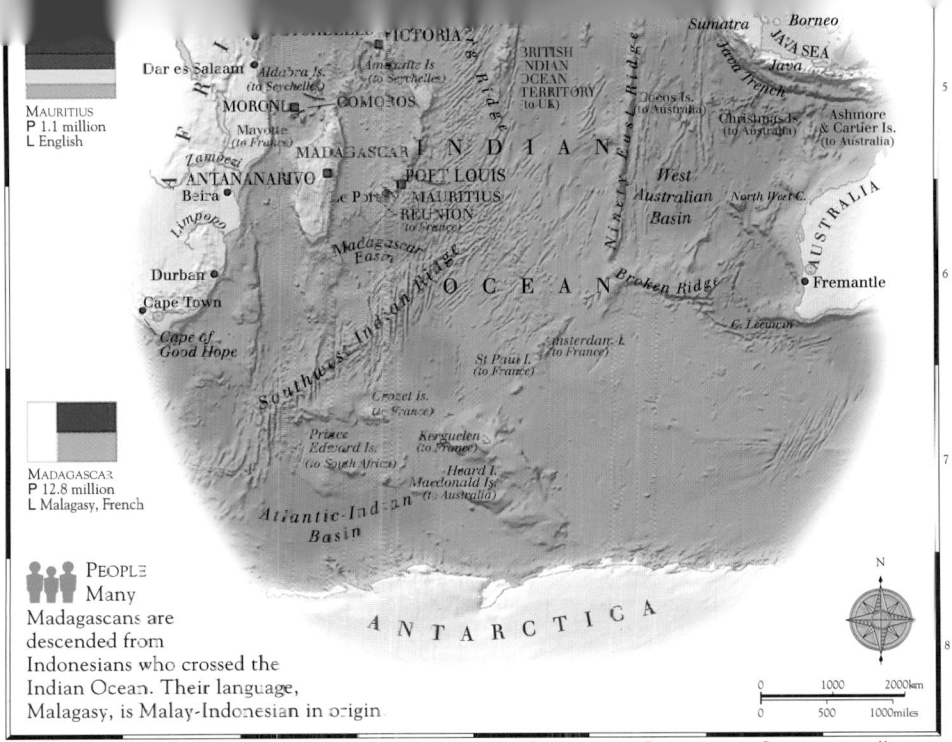
MAURITIUS
P 1.1 million
L English
MADAGASCAR
P 12.8 million
L Malagasy, French
PEOPLE
Many Madagascans are descended from Indonesians who crossed the Indian Ocean. Their language, Malagasy, is Malay-Indonesian in origin.
VICTORIA
Dar es Salaam
Aldabra Is. (to Seychelles)
Amirante Is (to Seychelles)
BRITISH INDIAN OCEAN TERRITORY (to UK)
MORONI
COMOROS
Mayotte (to France)
MADAGASCAR
INDIAN
OCEAN
PORT LOUIS
ANTANANARIVO
Beira
Le Port
MAURITIUS
REUNION (to France)
Zambezi
Limpopo
Madagascar Basin
Southwest Indian Ridge
Durban
Cape Town
Cape of Good Hope
Amsterdam I. (to France)
St Paul I. (to France)
Crozet Is. (to France)
Prince Edward Is. (to South Africa)
Kerguelen (to France)
Heard I.
Macdonald Is. (to Australia)
Atlantic-Indian Basin
ANTARCTICA
Sumatra
Borneo
JAVA SEA
Java
Java Trench
Cocos Is. (to Australia)
Christmas Is. (to Australia)
Ashmore & Cartier Is. (to Australia)
West Australian Basin
North West C.
AUSTRALIA
Broken Ridge
Fremantle
C. Leeuwin
N
0 1000 2000km
0 500 1000miles
A B C D E F G H
5 6 7 8

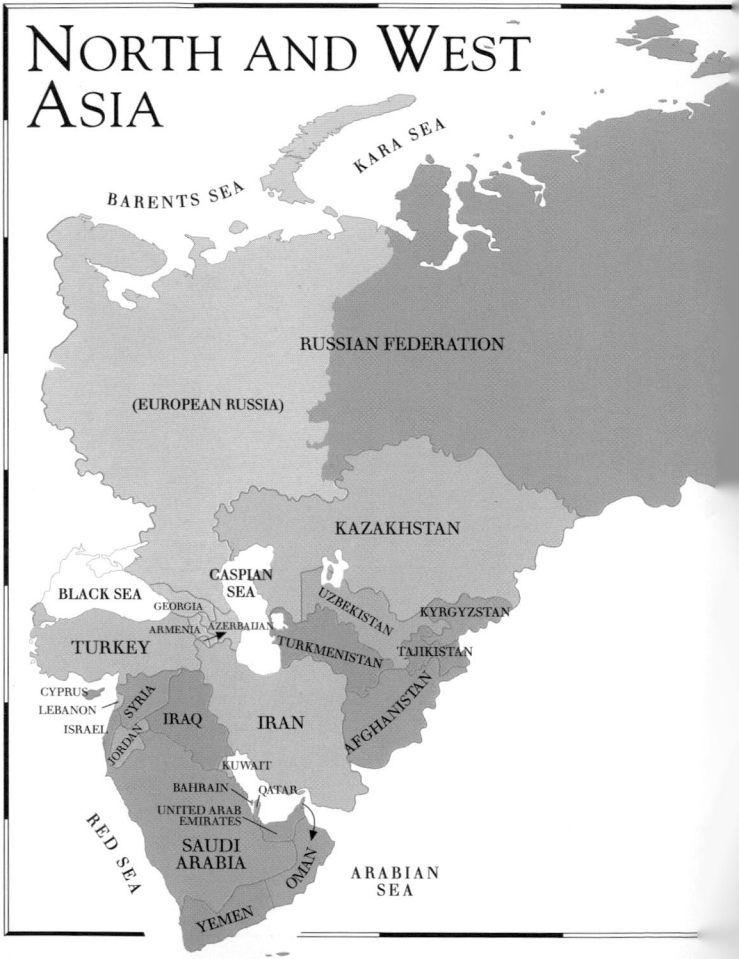
NORTH AND WEST ASIA
KARA SEA
BARENTS SEA
RUSSIAN FEDERATION
(EUROPEAN RUSSIA)
KAZAKHSTAN
CASPIAN SEA
BLACK SEA
GEORGIA
ARMENIA
AZERBAIJAN
UZBEKISTAN
KYRGYZSTAN
TURKMENISTAN
TAJIKISTAN
TURKEY
CYPRUS
LEBANON
ISRAEL
SYRIA
JORDAN
IRAQ
IRAN
AFGHANISTAN
KUWAIT
BAHRAIN
QATAR
UNITED ARAB EMIRATES
SAUDI ARABIA
OMAN
YEMEN
RED SEA
ARABIAN SEA

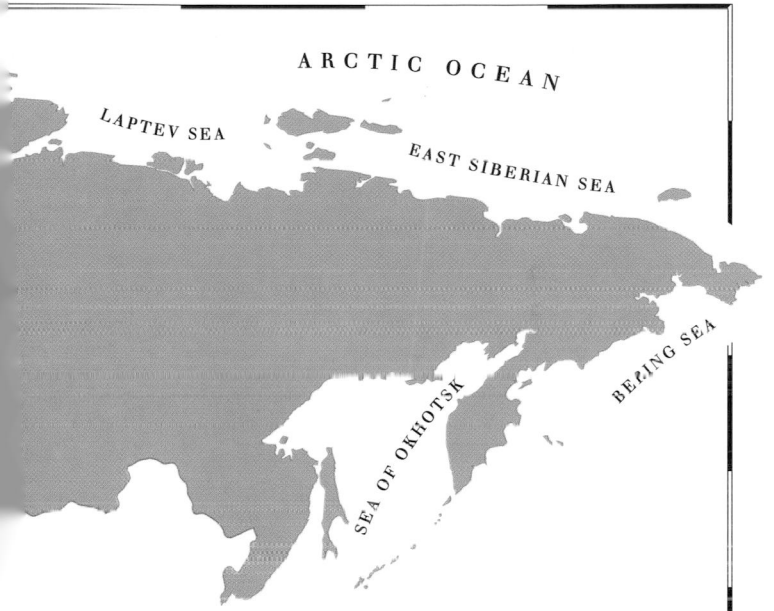

North and West Asia

Asia is the largest continent in the world, occupying nearly one-third of the world's total land area. In the south, the Arabian Peninsula is mostly hot, dry desert. In the north lie cold deserts, treeless plains called steppes, and the largest needleleaf forest in the world, which stretches from Siberia to northern Europe.

TURKEY AND CYPRUS

BRIDGING THE CONTINENTS of Europe and Asia, Turkey was once the centre of the Ottoman Empire, which controlled a quarter of Europe. Cyprus became independent from the UK in 1960, but was invaded by Turkey in 1974. Southern Cyprus is Greek; Northern Cyprus is still occupied by Turkey.

TURKEY
P 59.6 million
L Turkish

INDUSTRY
Wheat, corn, sugar beets, nuts, fruit, cotton, tobacco, tourism. Carpet-weaving is a centuries-old tradition. Figs and peaches are grown on the coast of the Mediterranean.

ENVIRONMENT
Turkey's dam-building projects on the Tigris and Euphrates Rivers have met with disapproval from Syria and Iraq, whose own rivers will have reduced flow as a result.

PEOPLE
The Kurds are Turkey's main minority group and one of the largest groups of stateless people in the world. Their homeland, Kurdistan, straddles three countries: Turkey, Iraq, and Iran. Kurds are fighting for the recognition of their rights within Turkey.

E F G H

NATURAL FEATURES
Turkey lies within the Alpine-Himalayan mountain belt. The Arabian, African, Eurasian, Aegean, and Turkish plates all converge within its borders, resulting in severe seismic activity.

CLIMATE
Coastal regions of Turkey and Cyprus have a Mediterranean climate. The Turkish interior has cold, snowy winters and hot, dry summers.

1

2

3

HISTORY
Greeks colonized the Aegean coast in 700 B.C. The Temple of Artemis in the city of Ephesus is one of the seven wonders of the ancient world.

CYPRUS
P 700,000
L Greek (Turkish)

N

0 150 300km
0 100 150miles

7

8

E F G H

THE NEAR EAST

AT THE JUNCTION of Africa, Asia, and Europe, the Near East is a mosaic of deserts, mountains, and fertile valleys. After centuries of conflict over territory, there is now some hope for peace in the region. In 1994, Israel and Jordan ended 46 years of hostility, and Israel withdrew from Gaza and Jericho. Israel and Palestine still struggle towards a negotiated peace, despite constant setbacks.

LEBANON
P 2.9 million
L Arabic

INDUSTRY
Oil, potash, cotton, fruit. Water is in short supply in this region and special irrigation techniques are used in order to avoid waste. Syria's main cash crop is cotton.

ISRAEL
P 5.4 million
L Hebrew, Arabic

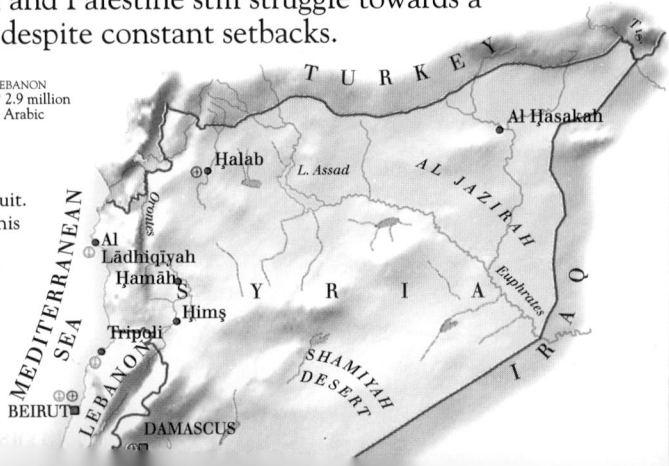

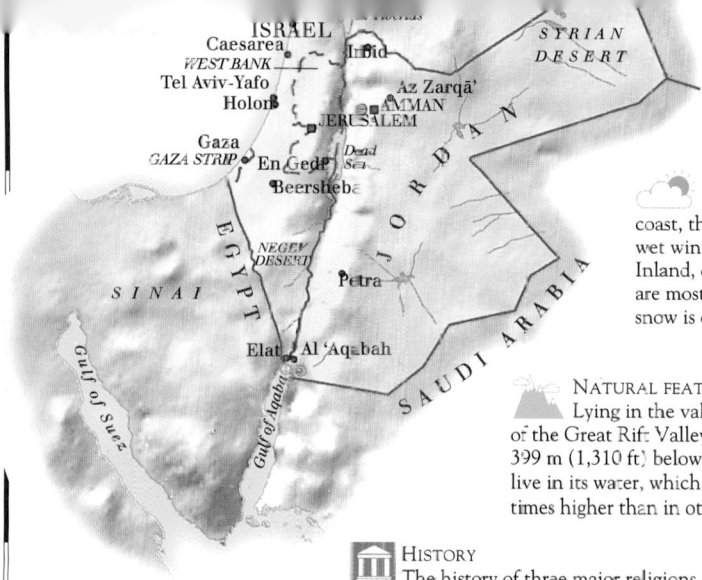

SYRIA
P 13.8 million
L Arabic

CLIMATE

On the Mediterranean coast, the climate is mild, with wet winters and hot, dry summers. Inland, countries in this region are mostly arid. In the mountains, snow is common in winter.

NATURAL FEATURES

Lying in the valley that forms a part of the Great Rift Valley, the Dead Sea is 399 m (1,310 ft) below sea level. No fish live in its water, which has salt levels six times higher than in other seas.

HISTORY

The history of three major religions – Judaism, Islam, and Christianity – is bound up in the city of Jerusalem. The city contains holy sites such as the Wailing Wall, the Dome of the Rock, and the Church of the Holy Sepulchre.

JORDAN
P 4.4 million
L Arabic

THE MIDDLE EAST

ISLAM WAS FOUNDED in A.D. 570 in Mecca, Saudi Arabia, and spread throughout the Middle East, where today it is the main religion. Oil has brought wealth to the region but in 1991, the area was devastated by the Gulf War.

IRAQ
P 19.9 million
L Arabic

INDUSTRY
Oil, natural gas, fishing, carpet-weaving, offshore banking. Saudi Arabia has the world's largest oil reserves. Over 60 per cent of the world's desalination plants are used in this region to make sea water drinkable.

SAUDI ARABIA
P 16.5 million
L Arabic

KUWAIT
P 1.8 million
L Arabic

BAHRAIN
P 500,000
L Arabic

QATAR
P 500,000
L Arabic

CLIMATE
Most of the countries in this region are semi-arid, with low rainfall. Inland, summer temperatures can reach 48°C (119°F) with winter temperatures falling to freezing.

HISTORY
Ancient civilizations developed about 5,500 years ago in Mesopotamia, between the Tigris and Euphrates Rivers. The Sumerian civilization had advanced methods of irrigation, sophisticated architecture, and a form of writing called cuneiform.

UNITED ARAB EMIRATES
P 1.7 million
L Arabic

YEMEN
P 13 million
L Arabic

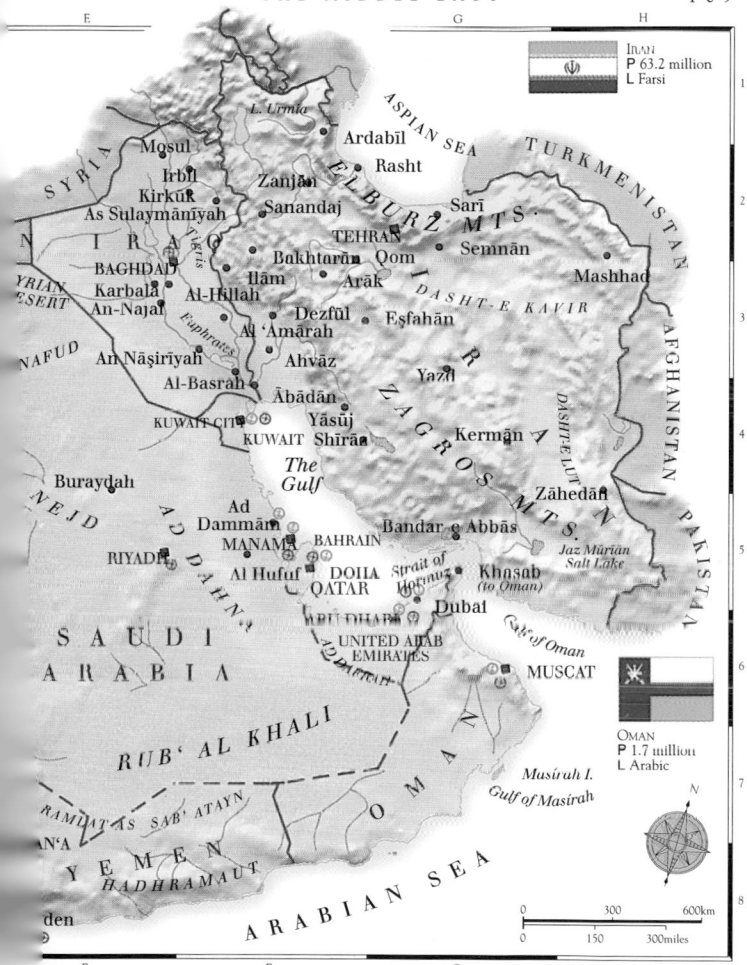
E
G
H
Iran
P 63.2 million
L Farsi
L. Urmia
Ardabīl
Rasht
ASPIAN SEA
TURKMENISTAN
SYRIA
Mosul
Irbil
Kirkūk
Zanjān
Sanandaj
As Sulaymānīyah
ELBURZ MTS.
Sarī
TEHRAN
Semnān
Mashhad
IRAQ
Tigris
Bakhtarān
Qom
BAGHDAD
Ilām
Arāk
DASHT-E KAVIR
Karbalā
Al-Hillah
An-Najaf
Euphrates
Dezfūl
Eṣfahān
AFGHANISTAN
Al 'Amārah
Ahvāz
An Nāṣirīyah
Al-Basrah
Yazd
Ābādān
KUWAIT CITY
Yāsūj
KUWAIT
Shīrāz
Kermān
ZAGROS MTS.
DASHT-E LUT
The Gulf
Buraydah
Zāhedān
Ad Dammām
Bandar e Abbās
BAHRAIN
MANAMA
RIYADH
Al Hufuf
DOHA
QATAR
Strait of Hormuz
Khasab
(to Oman)
Jaz Mūrian Salt Lake
PAKISTAN
Dubai
ABU DHABI
UNITED ARAB EMIRATES
Gulf of Oman
MUSCAT
SAUDI ARABIA
RUB' AL KHALI
OMAN
Masirah I.
Gulf of Masirah
RAMLAT AS SAB' ATAYN
YEMEN
HADHRAMAUT
ARABIAN SEA
Oman
P 1.7 million
L Arabic
N
0 300 600km
0 150 300miles

CENTRAL ASIA

FOR CENTURIES, many people in central Asia lived in mountains as nomads, or in cities that sprung up along the Silk Road. When the region came under Soviet rule, industry was developed and irrigation schemes made farming possible.

USTYURT PLATEAU
ARAL SEA
TURAN LOWLAND
L. Sarykamysh
Nukus
UZBE
Zaliv Kara-Bogaz-Gol
Tashauz
Urgench
CASPIAN SEA
Krasnovodsk
Nebit Dag
TURKMENISTAN
ASHKABAD
Karakum
Murgab
Tedzhen
IRAN
Her
AF

INDUSTRY

Cotton, gold, gas, sulphur, mercury, opium, hydroelectricity. Uzbekistan has the largest single gold mine in the world. Tajikistan has 14 per cent of the world's known uranium resources.

HISTORY

In the early 1900s, most of this region, except for Afghanistan, came under Soviet rule, which restricted the use of local languages and Islam. Today, these newly independent countries are resuming the religions, languages, and traditions of their past.

TURKMENISTAN
P 4 million
L Turkmen, Russian

ENVIRONMENT

Crop irrigation draws water from the Amu Darya river, reducing the amount of water flowing into the Aral Sea. By the year 2000, the Sea will have shrunk to an estimated third of its original size.

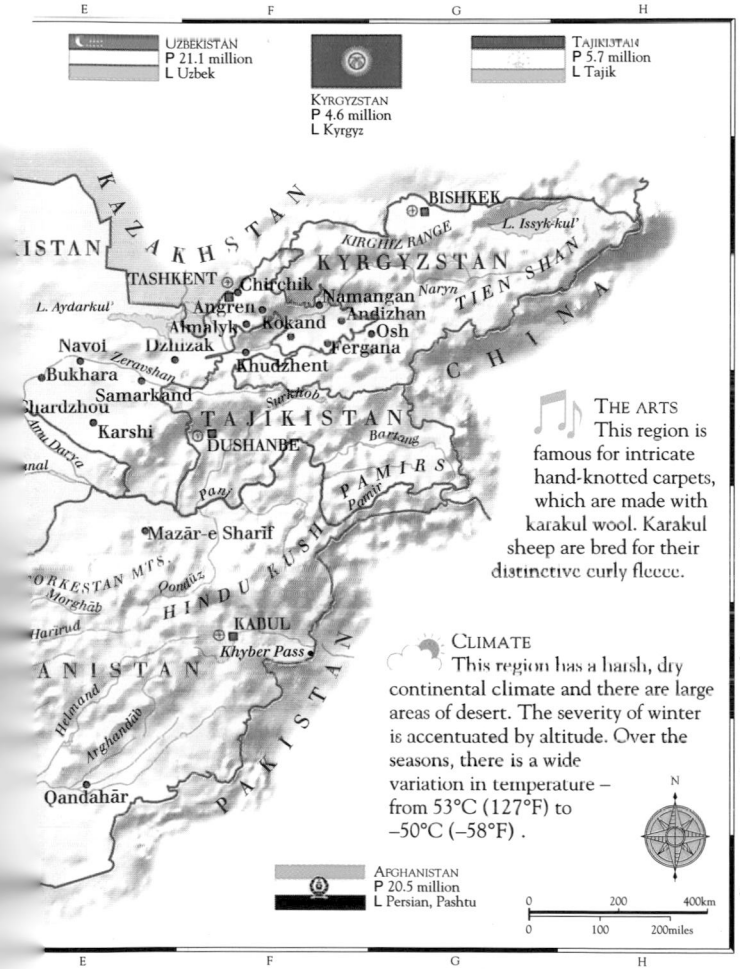

THE ARTS

This region is famous for intricate hand-knotted carpets, which are made with karakul wool. Karakul sheep are bred for their distinctive curly fleece.

CLIMATE

This region has a harsh, dry continental climate and there are large areas of desert. The severity of winter is accentuated by altitude. Over the seasons, there is a wide variation in temperature – from 53°C (127°F) to –50°C (–58°F) .

THE RUSSIAN FEDERATION AND KAZAKHSTAN

EXTENDING FROM the frozen north to the central Asian deserts in the south, the Ural Mountains separate European and Asian Russia. Independent since 1991, Kazakhstan is one of the most underpopulated countries in the world.

CLIMATE

Kazakhstan has a continental climate. Winter temperatures in Russia vary little from north to south, but fall sharply in the east, especially in Siberia.

PEOPLE

There are 57 nationalities with their own territories within the Russian Federation. A further 95 groups have no territories of their own, although these groups make up only six per cent of the population.

FINLAND
Murmansk
BARENTS SEA
ESTONIA
LATVIA
St. Petersburg
Pskov
Novgorod
Arkhangel'sk
BELORUSSIA
Smolensk
MOSCOW
Yaroslavl'
UKRAINE
Tula
Ryazan'
Kirov
URAL MOUNTAINS
Voronezh
Penza
Kazan'
Izhevsk
Perm'
Irtysh
Rostov-na-Donu
Simbirsk
Naberezhnyye Chelny
Saratov
Samara
Tol'yatti
Yekaterinburg
Krasnodar
Volgograd
Ufa
Chelyabinsk
Ural'sk
Orenburg
GEORGIA
Astrakhan
Ural
Omsk
Aktyubinsk
Kustanai
Atyrau
Ashim
Grozny
Emba
ASTANA
CASPIAN SEA
KIRGHIZ STEPPE
L. Tengiz
UZBEKISTAN
ARAL SEA
Karaganda
KAZAKHSTAN
Kzyl-Orda
Syr Darya
L. Balkha
TURKMENISTAN
UZBEKISTAN
Chu
Shymkent
Almaty

KAZAKHSTAN
P 17.2 million
L Kazakh

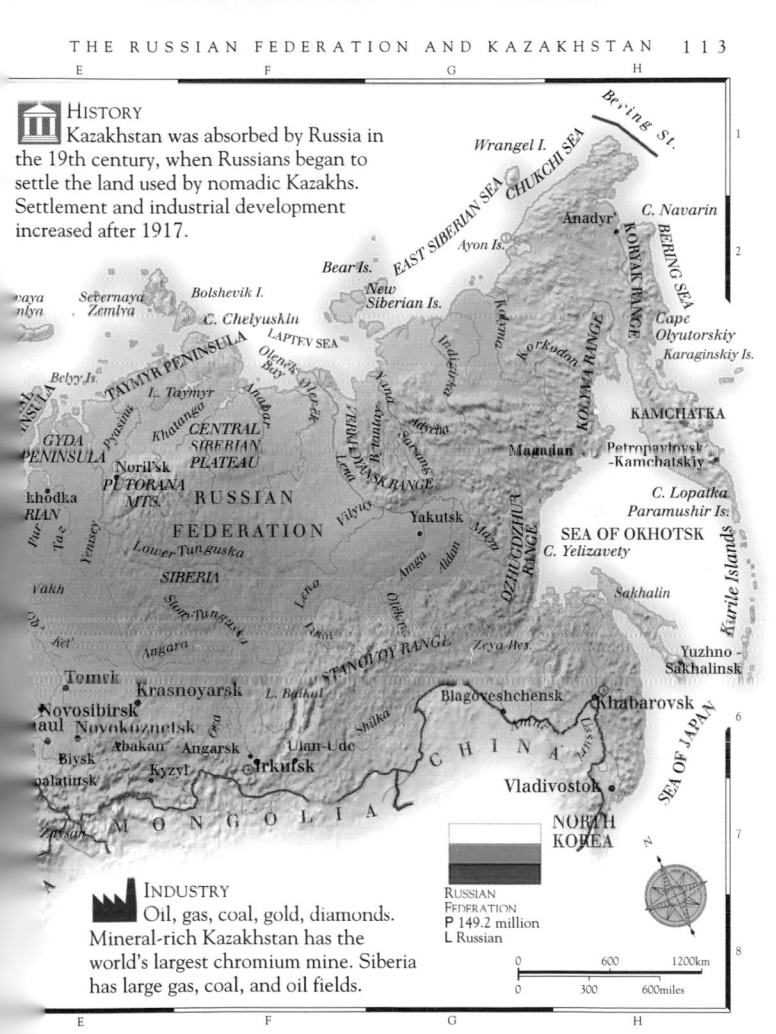
HISTORY
Kazakhstan was absorbed by Russia in the 19th century, when Russians began to settle the land used by nomadic Kazakhs. Settlement and industrial development increased after 1917.
INDUSTRY
Oil, gas, coal, gold, diamonds. Mineral-rich Kazakhstan has the world's largest chromium mine. Siberia has large gas, coal, and oil fields.
RUSSIAN FEDERATION
P 149.2 million
L Russian
Bering St.
Wrangel I.
CHUKCHI SEA
EAST SIBERIAN SEA
Anadyr'
C. Navarin
KORYAK RANGE
BERING SEA
Ayon Is.
Bear Is.
New Siberian Is.
Severnaya Zemlya
Bolshevik I.
C. Chelyuskin
LAPTEV SEA
Kolyma
Korkodon
KOLYMA RANGE
Cape Olyutorskiy
Karaginskiy Is.
Belyy Is.
TAYMYR PENINSULA
L. Taymyr
Olenyok Bay
Olenyok
Anabar
Yana
Indigirka
Khatanga
CENTRAL SIBERIAN PLATEAU
GYDA PENINSULA
Noril'sk
PUTORANA MTS.
VERKHOYANSK RANGE
Aldyrma
Sakhalin
Magadan
KAMCHATKA
Petropavlovsk -Kamchatskiy
C. Lopatka
Paramushir Is.
RUSSIAN FEDERATION
Lena
Vilyuy
Yakutsk
Maya
Aldan
Amga
DZHUGDZHUR RANGE
SEA OF OKHOTSK
C. Yelizavety
Kurile Islands
Yenisey
Taz
Lower Tunguska
SIBERIA
Vakh
Stony Tunguska
Angara
Olekma
Zeya Res.
STANOVOY RANGE
Sakhalin
Yuzhno-Sakhalinsk
Tomsk
Novosibirsk
Krasnoyarsk
L. Baikal
Blagoveshchensk
Khabarovsk
Novokuznetsk
Abakan
Angarsk
Ulan-Ude
Biysk
Kyzyl
Irkutsk
Shilka
Amur
Ussuri
CHINA
Vladivostok
SEA OF JAPAN
MONGOLIA
NORTH KOREA
N
0 600 1200km
0 300 600miles

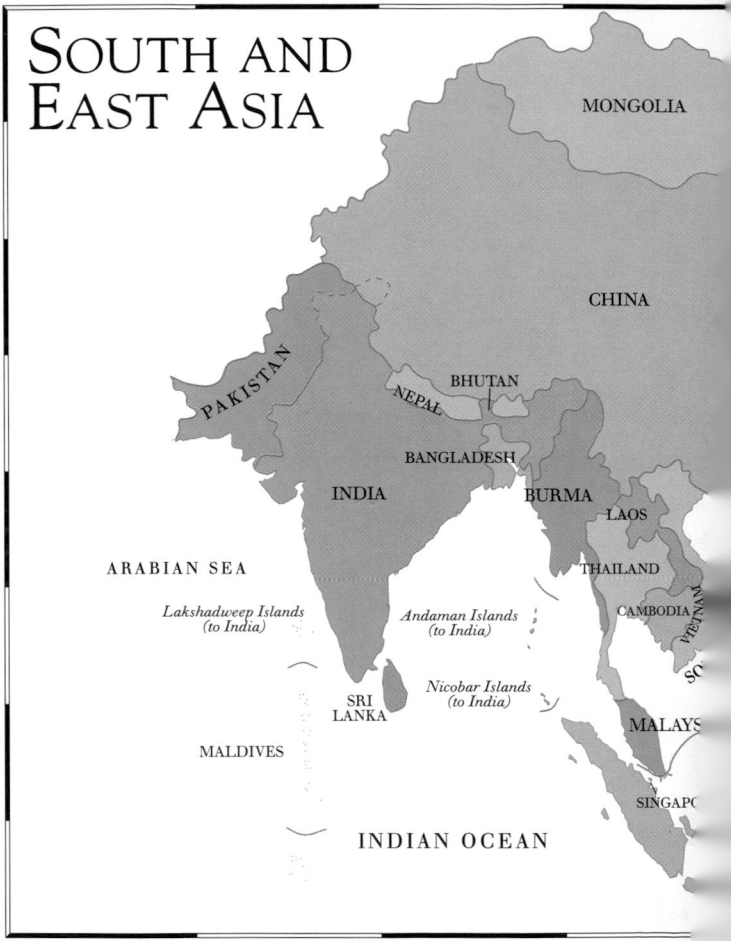
SOUTH AND
EAST ASIA
MONGOLIA
CHINA
PAKISTAN
NEPAL
BHUTAN
BANGLADESH
INDIA
BURMA
LAOS
THAILAND
CAMBODIA
ARABIAN SEA
Lakshadweep Islands
(to India)
Andaman Islands
(to India)
Nicobar Islands
(to India)
SRI
LANKA
MALDIVES
INDIAN OCEAN

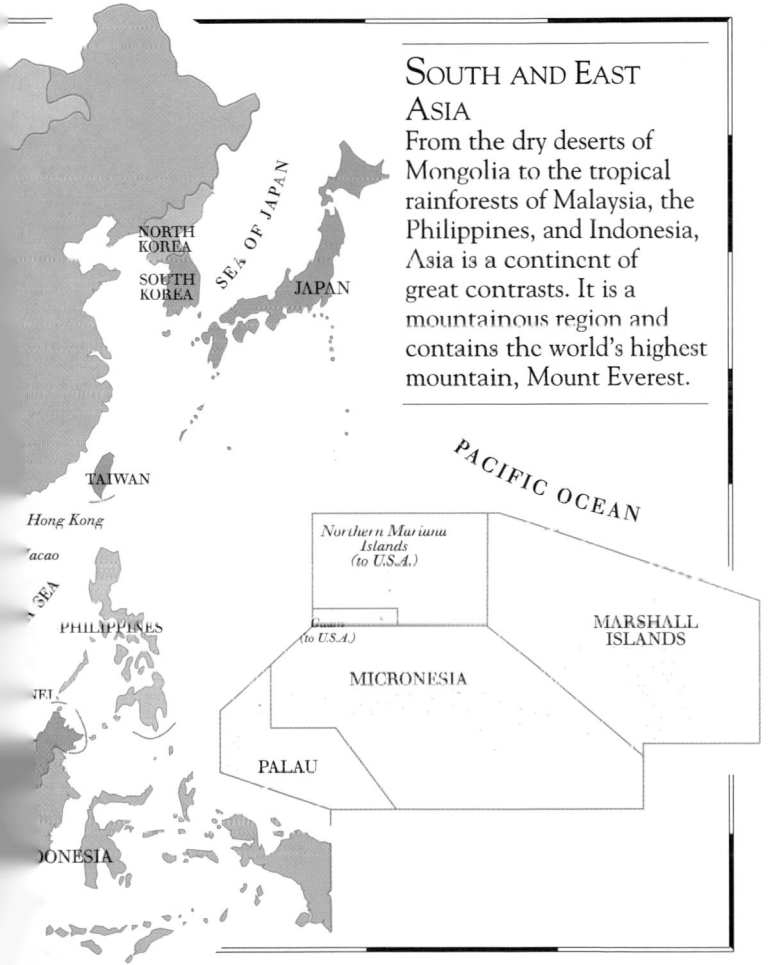

South and East Asia

From the dry deserts of Mongolia to the tropical rainforests of Malaysia, the Philippines, and Indonesia, Asia is a continent of great contrasts. It is a mountainous region and contains the world's highest mountain, Mount Everest.

THE INDIAN SUBCONTINENT

SEPARATED FROM THE rest of Asia by the Himalayas, India is the second most populated country after China. It is estimated that India's population will overtake that of China by 2030. To the north, Nepal and Bhutan lie nestled in the Himalayas between China and India. To the south lies Sri Lanka, once known as Ceylon.

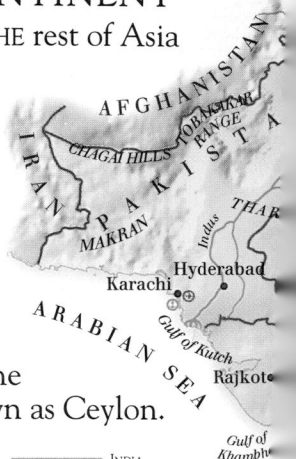

INDIA
P 896.6 million
L Hindi, English

INDUSTRY
Tea, jute, iron, cut diamonds, cotton, rice, sugar cane, textiles. Bangladesh exports 80 per cent of the world's jute fibre. Sri Lanka is the largest tea exporter in the world. Pakistan is a major exporter of rice.

HISTORY
In 1947, when India gained independence, religious differences led to the creation of two countries – Hindu India and Muslim Pakistan. In 1971, a short civil war broke out between East and West Pakistan and East Pakistan became Bangladesh.

NATURAL FEATURES
The Himalayas were formed as a result of a violent crumpling of the Earth's crust. Frequent earthquakes indicate that the process is continuing. The highest peaks in the world, including Mount Everest, are in this mountain system.

N

0 350 700
0 200 400m

G
H
PAKISTAN
P 128.1 million
L Urdu
NEPAL
P 21.1 million
L Nepali
BHUTAN
P 1.7 million
L Dzongkha
BANGLADESH
P 122.2 million
L Bengali
SRI LANKA
P 17.9 million
L Sinhalese, Tamil
CLIMATE
Sri Lanka and southern India are tropical, with little seasonal variation in temperature. The north has a cold alpine climate. Cyclones regularly build up in the Bay of Bengal, and Bangladesh is often flooded during the monsoon.
ISLAMABAD
Srinagar
Gujranwala
Lahore
Amritsar
Jalandhar
Ludhiana
Chandigarh
Meerut
NEW DELHI
Bareilly
Jaipur
Agra
Gwalior
Lucknow
KATHMANDU
THIMPHU
BHUTAN
Brahmaputra
Guwahati
Kota
Kanpur
Varanasi
Patna
Imphal
Allahabad
Gandi Res.
Rajshahi
BANGLADESH
Bhopal
Jabalpur
Dhanbad
DACCA
Agartala
Indore
Narmada
Ranchi
Calcutta
Khulna
Chittagong
Nagpur
Tapti
Nasik
Thane
Mahanadi
Godavari
DECCAN
Pune
Sholapur
EASTERN GHATS
Vishakhapatnam
Hyderabad
PLATEAU
Vijayawada
Dharwad
COROMANDEL COAST
Bay of Bengal
Mangalore
Bangalore
Madras
Coimbatore
Cochin
Madurai
Jaffna
SRI LANKA
COLOMBO
Galle
CHINA
NEPAL
INDIA
BURMA

CHINA AND MONGOLIA

ISOLATED FROM THE western world for centuries, the Chinese were the first to develop the compass, paper, gunpowder, porcelain, and silk. Three autonomous regions lie within western China – Inner Mongolia, Xinjiang, and Tibet. The Gobi desert in vast Mongolia is the world's most northern desert.

PEOPLE

Han Chinese make up 93 per cent of China's population. China has relaxed its 1979 one-child policy for minority groups, such as the Mongolians, Tibetans, and Muslim Uygurs, after some groups faced near extinction.

HISTORY

Tibet was invaded by China in 1950. The Chinese destroyed Tibet's traditional agricultural society and brutally repressed Buddhism. In 1959 there were more than 6,000 Buddhist monasteries – by 1980, only 179 remained.

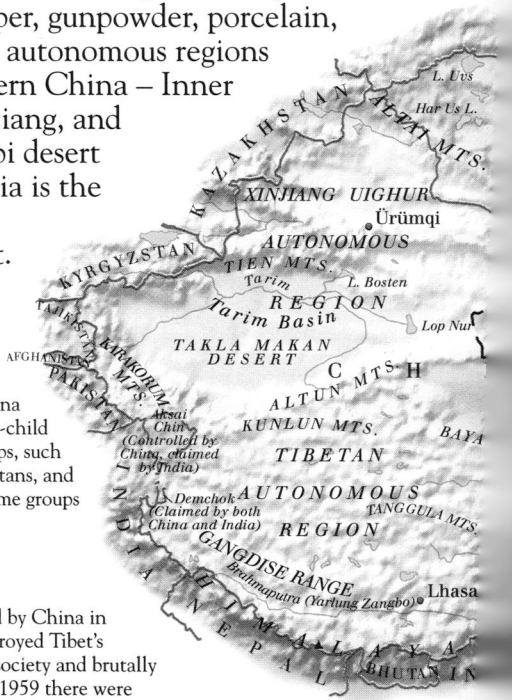

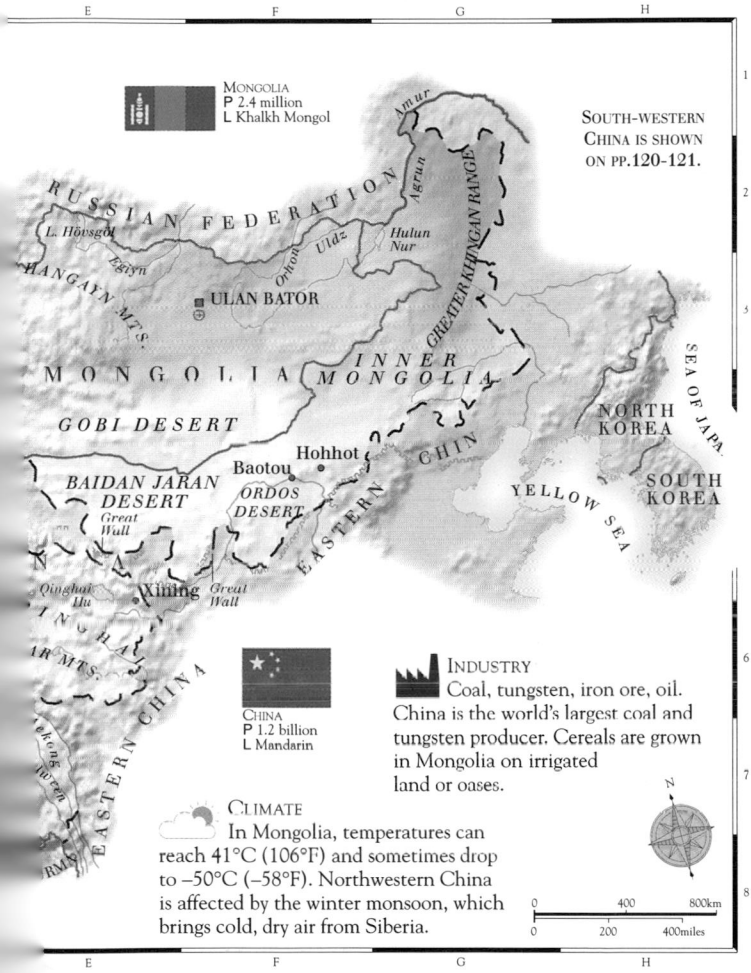
E
F
G
H
1
2
3
6
7
8
MONGOLIA
P 2.4 million
L Khalkh Mongol
SOUTH-WESTERN CHINA IS SHOWN ON PP.120-121.
Amur
Argun
GREATER KHINGAN RANGE
RUSSIAN FEDERATION
L. Hövsgöl
Hulun Nur
Orhon
Uldz
Eginyn
HANGAIN MTS.
ULAN BATOR
MONGOLIA
INNER MONGOLIA
GOBI DESERT
SEA OF JAPAN
NORTH KOREA
Hohhot
Baotou
CHIN
BAIDAN JARAN DESERT
Great Wall
ORDOS DESERT
EASTERN
YELLOW SEA
SOUTH KOREA
Qinghai Hu
Xining
Great Wall
AR MTS.
EASTERN CHINA
CHINA
P 1.2 billion
L Mandarin
INDUSTRY
Coal, tungsten, iron ore, oil. China is the world's largest coal and tungsten producer. Cereals are grown in Mongolia on irrigated land or oases.
CLIMATE
In Mongolia, temperatures can reach 41°C (106°F) and sometimes drop to –50°C (–58°F). Northwestern China is affected by the winter monsoon, which brings cold, dry air from Siberia.
N
0 400 800km
0 200 400miles

CHINA AND KOREA

ONE-FIFTH OF the world's population lives in China – mostly in the eastern part of the country. Annexed to Japan in 1910, Korea was divided between the U.S.A. and Communist Russia after World War II. North and South Korea were formed in 1948.

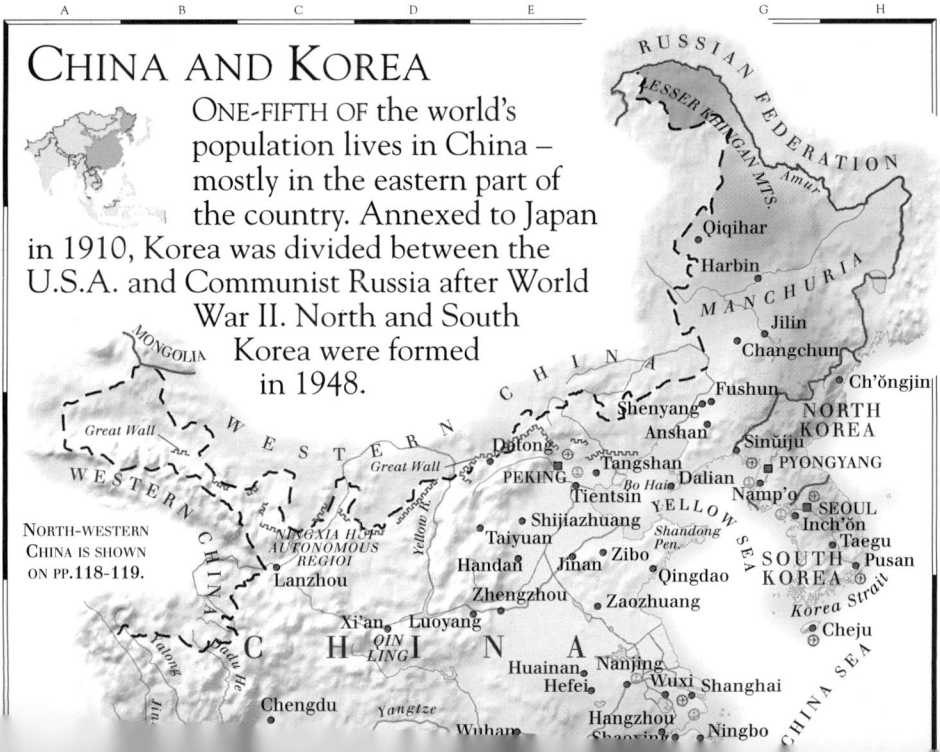

NORTH-WESTERN CHINA IS SHOWN ON PP.118-119.

NORTH KOREA
P 23.1 million
L Korean

SOUTH KOREA
P 44.5 million
L Korean

TAIWAN
P 20.8 million
L Mandarin

CHINA
P 1.2 billion
L Mandarin

PEOPLE

Korea has been inhabited by one ethnic group for 2,000 years and even today those with the same surname group may not marry each other. Most Taiwanese are descendants of the Chinese supporters of the deposed Ming dynasty, who migrated in 1644.

0 300 600km
0 150 300miles

CLIMATE

Southern South Korea and Taiwan have a tropical monsoon climate similar to that of southern China. North Korea has a continental climate.

HISTORY

On 1 July, 1997, Britain returned Hong Kong to China where it is now run as a Special Administrative Region.

COMMUNICATIONS

South Korea has one of the world's best public transport systems. Buses, trains, boats, and planes are all integrated in one timetable.

INDUSTRY

Rice, electronics, wheat, finance, textiles. Hong Kong has the busiest container port in the world. Taiwan is the world's leading producer of watches, computers, televisions, and track shoes.

JAPAN

CONSISTING OF FOUR main islands and 4,000 smaller ones, Japan is the world's leading industrial nation. Since two-thirds of the land is mountainous, the majority of people live on the coast. Japan has about 1,500 minor earthquakes a year, but severe earthquakes, such as the one in Kobe in 1994, occur every few years. Underwater earthquakes sometimes cause huge surge waves, or *tsunami*, along Japan's Pacific coast.

INDUSTRY

Fishing, ship building, motor vehicles, computers, televisions, high-tech electronics. Motor vehicles are Japan's biggest export, and its stock exchange ranks second in the world. Japan excels at producing miniature electronic goods.

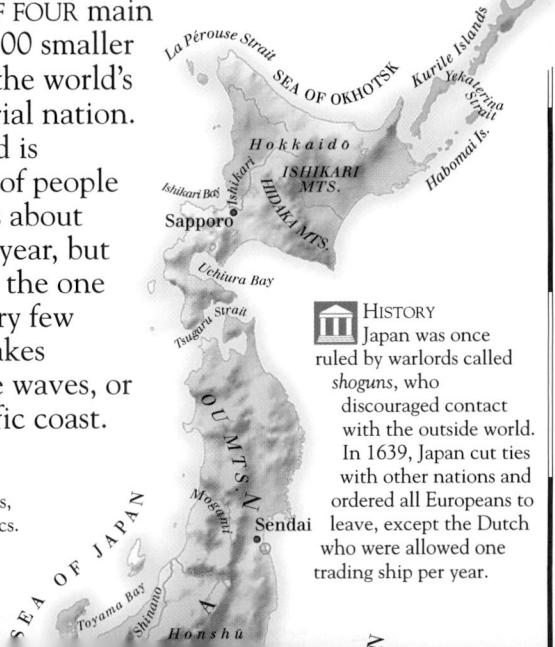

HISTORY

Japan was once ruled by warlords called *shoguns*, who discouraged contact with the outside world. In 1639, Japan cut ties with other nations and ordered all Europeans to leave, except the Dutch who were allowed one trading ship per year.

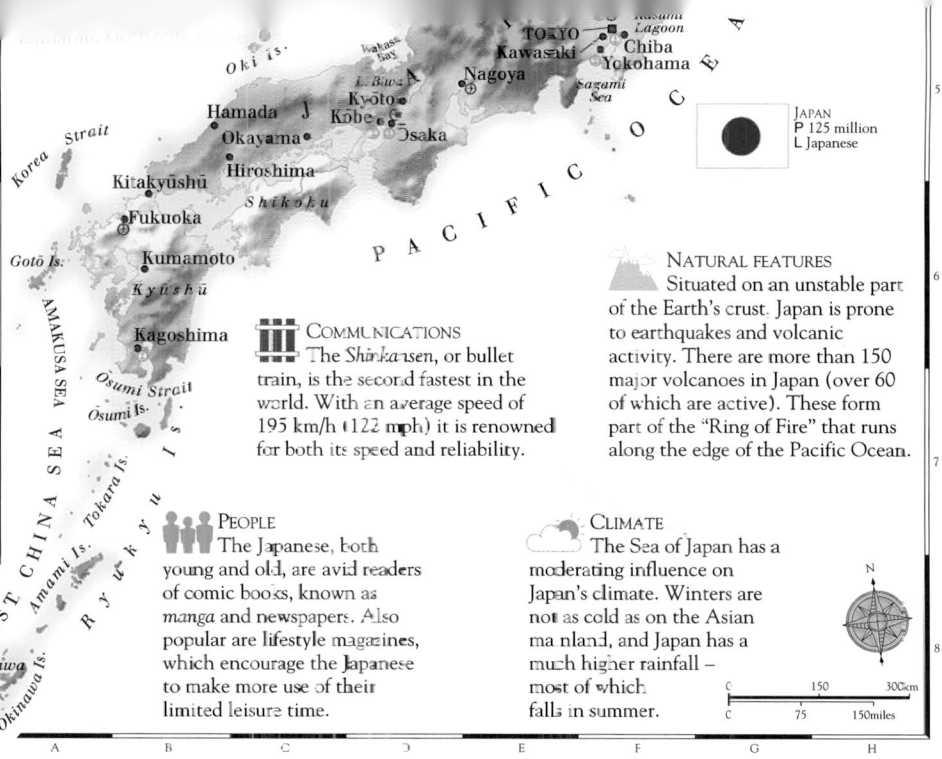

Communications

The *Shinkansen*, or bullet train, is the second fastest in the world. With an average speed of 195 km/h (122 mph) it is renowned for both its speed and reliability.

People

The Japanese, both young and old, are avid readers of comic books, known as *manga* and newspapers. Also popular are lifestyle magazines, which encourage the Japanese to make more use of their limited leisure time.

Natural features

Situated on an unstable part of the Earth's crust, Japan is prone to earthquakes and volcanic activity. There are more than 150 major volcanoes in Japan (over 60 of which are active). These form part of the "Ring of Fire" that runs along the edge of the Pacific Ocean.

Climate

The Sea of Japan has a moderating influence on Japan's climate. Winters are not as cold as on the Asian mainland, and Japan has a much higher rainfall – most of which falls in summer.

MAINLAND SOUTHEAST ASIA

FOR MOST OF its history, Thailand has been an independent kingdom. Malaysia includes 11 states on the mainland (Malaya), as well as Sabah and Sarawak in Borneo. Cambodia, Laos, and Vietnam have suffered from years of civil war. Burma has become more and more isolated from the world by its repressive government.

BURMA (MYANMAR)
P 44.6 million
L Burmese (Myanmar)

LAOS
P 4.6 million
L Lao

INDIA
CHINA
BURMA
LAOS
VIETNAM
B'DESH
Bay of Bengal
Gulf of Tongking
KUMON RANGE
CHIN HILLS
Chindwin
Irrawaddy
Salween
Sittang
Mekong
Nam Ou
Black R.
Red R.
Nam Theun
L. Thac Ba
L. Inle
Monywa
Mandalay
Sagaing
Amarapura
Pakokku
Minbu
Taunggyi
Pyinmana
Prome
Sandoway
Chiang Mai
Louang Phrabang
Viet Tri
HANOI
Thai Nguyen
Hong Gai
Hai Phong
Nam Dinh
Thanh Hoa
Vinh

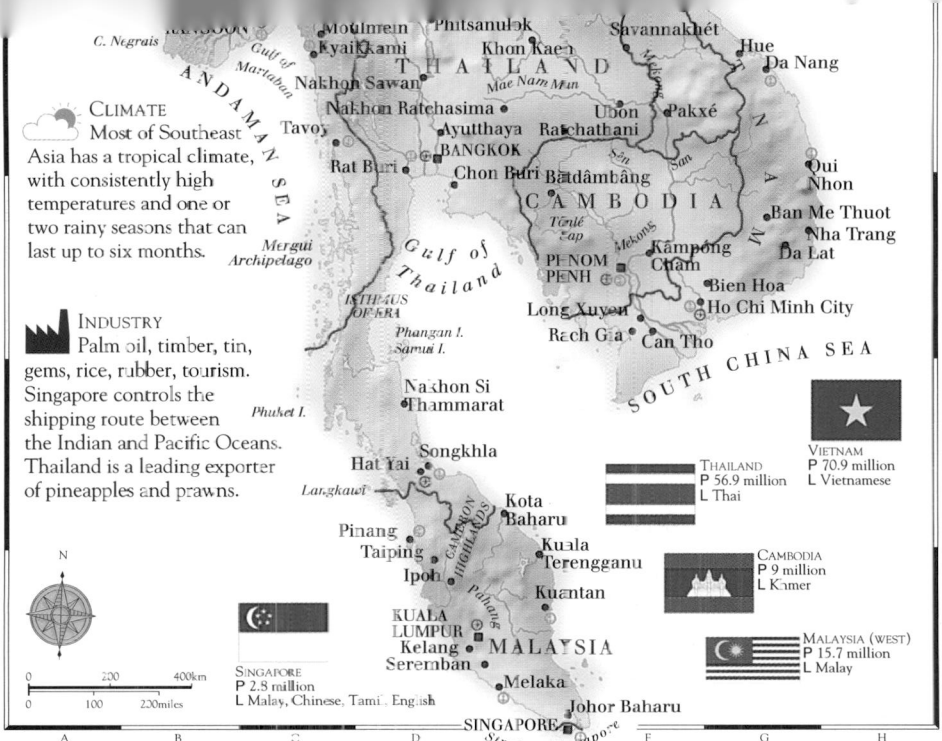

Climate

Most of Southeast Asia has a tropical climate, with consistently high temperatures and one or two rainy seasons that can last up to six months.

Industry

Palm oil, timber, tin, gems, rice, rubber, tourism. Singapore controls the shipping route between the Indian and Pacific Oceans. Thailand is a leading exporter of pineapples and prawns.

Thailand
P 56.9 million
L Thai

Vietnam
P 70.9 million
L Vietnamese

Cambodia
P 9 million
L Kamer

Malaysia (West)
P 15.7 million
L Malay

Singapore
P 2.8 million
L Malay, Chinese, Tamil, English

MARITIME SOUTHEAST ASIA

SCATTERED BETWEEN the Indian and Pacific Oceans are thousands of tropical mountainous islands. Once called the East Indies, Indonesia was ruled by the Dutch for 350 years. More than half of its 13,677 islands are still uninhabited. The Philippines lie on the "Ring of Fire", and are subject to earthquakes and volcanic activity. Borneo is shared among Indonesia, Malaysia, and Brunei.

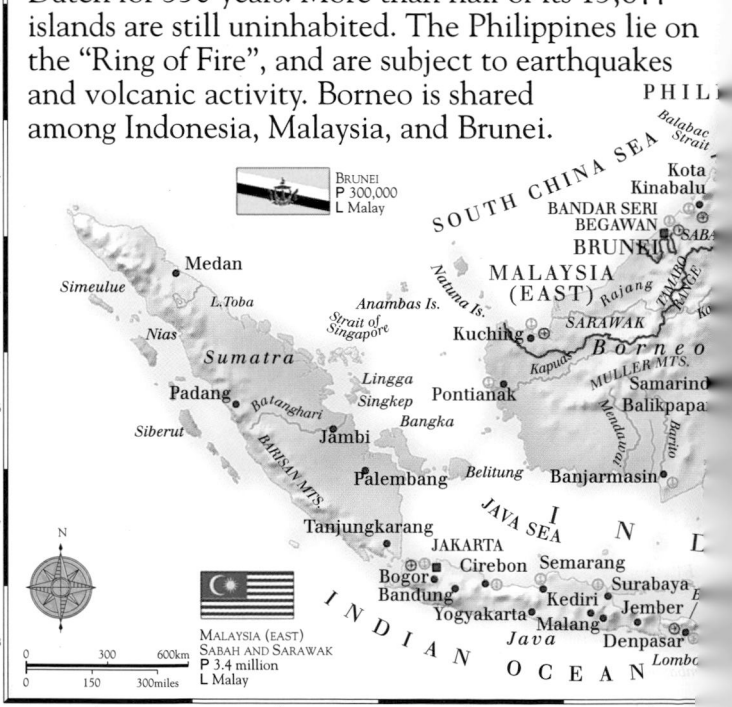

F
G
H
1
2
3
4
5
8
Luzon Strait
Luzon
PHILIPPINES
P 66.5 million
L Filipino, English
INDUSTRY
Palm oil, timber, rice, oil, natural gas, copper, chrome, tourism. Malaysia is the largest producer of palm oil and computer disk-drives. Indonesia is a major exporter of natural gas.
ENVIRONMENT
Logging, especially in Borneo and the Philippines, is a problem in the region. Forest communities, like the Malaysian Penan, are being destroyed. Some tree species are near extinction.
CLIMATE
Countries situated around the equator are hot and humid all year. Variations in climate are related to latitude.
Baguio
Dagupan
Cabanatuan
MANILA
Lucena
Naga
Legaspi
Mindoro
Mindoro Strait
Calbayog
Samar
Panay
Cadiz
Iloilo
Tacloban
Bacolod
Cebu
Negros
Butuan
Cagayan de Oro
Iligan
Mindanao
Zamboanga
Davao
Jolo
General Santos
Sulu Archipelago
Talaud Is.
PHILIPPINE SEA
PACIFIC OCEAN
CELEBES SEA
MOLUCCA SEA
Manado
Halmahera
Supiori
Biak
Jayapura
Gulf of Tomini
Moluccas
Sula Is.
Palu
Celebes
SERAM SEA
Mamberamo
IRIAN JAYA
MAOKE MTS.
Seram
Buru
Ambon
Kendari
ARAFURA SEA
Kai Is.
Aru Is.
Digul
BANDA SEA
Ujung Pandang
Dolak
Tanimbar Is.
PAPUA NEW GUINEA
FLORES SEA
Flores
Timor
Kupang
Roti
TIMOR SEA
INDONESIA
P 194.6 million
L Bahasa Indonesia

PACIFIC OCEAN

THE LARGEST AND deepest ocean, the Pacific covers a greater area of the Earth's surface than all the land areas together. Its deepest point – 11,033 m (36,197ft) – is deep enough to cover Mount Everest. Melanesia, Micronesia, and Polynesia are the main inner Pacific island groups.

MICRONESIA
P 101,000
L English

NAURU
P 10,000
L Nauruan, English

NATURAL FEATURES
Some Pacific islands are coral atolls – ring-shaped islands or chains of islands surrounding a lagoon. They are formed when coral builds up on a sunken bank or on a volcano crater in the open sea.

SOLOMON ISLANDS
P 400,000
L English

VANUATU
P 155,000
L Bislama, English, French

ENVIRONMENT
Nuclear testing by the U.S.A. and France has dangerously polluted areas in the South Pacific. Countries such as Japan, Australia, and New Zealand want the region made into a nuclear-free zone.

FIJI
P 700,000
L English

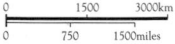

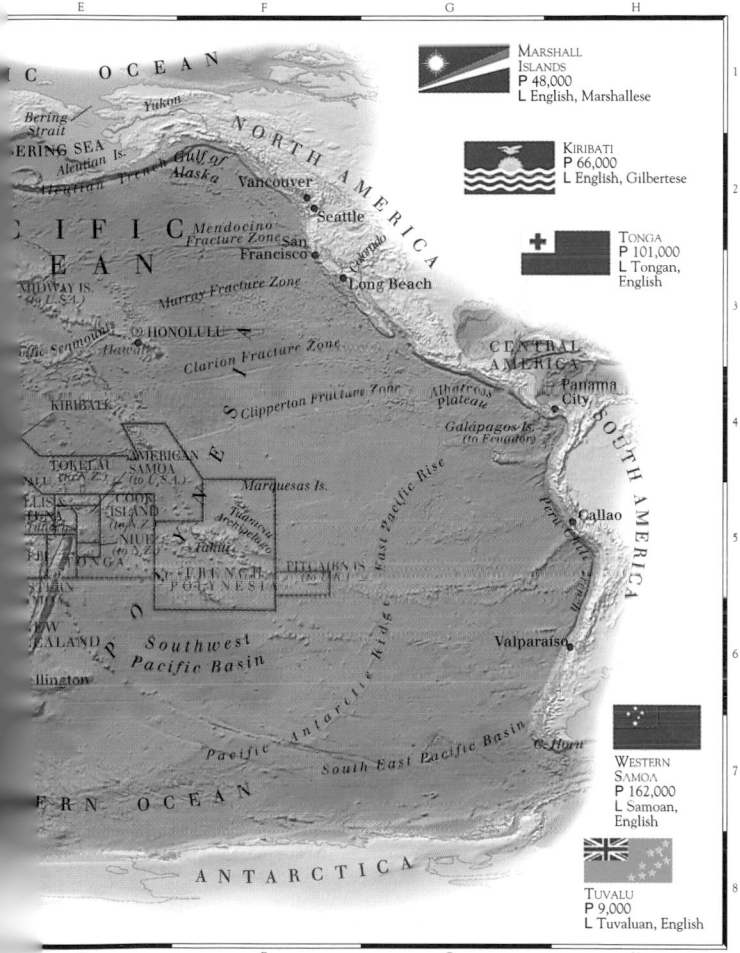
E F G H
1 2 3 4 5 6 7 8
MARSHALL ISLANDS
P 48,000
L English, Marshallese
KIRIBATI
P 66,000
L English, Gilbertese
TONGA
P 101,000
L Tongan, English
WESTERN SAMOA
P 162,000
L Samoan, English
TUVALU
P 9,000
L Tuvaluan, English
OCEAN
Bering Strait
BERING SEA
Aleutian Is.
Aleutian Trench
Gulf of Alaska
Yukon
NORTH AMERICA
Vancouver
Seattle
Mendocino Fracture Zone
San Francisco
Colorado
Long Beach
PACIFIC OCEAN
MIDWAY IS. (to U.S.A.)
Murray Fracture Zone
HONOLULU
Hawaii
Clarion Fracture Zone
CENTRAL AMERICA
Panama City
Albatross Plateau
Clipperton Fracture Zone
KIRIBATI
Galápagos Is. (to Ecuador)
SOUTH AMERICA
TOKELAU (to N.Z.)
AMERICAN SAMOA (to U.S.A.)
Marquesas Is.
COOK ISLANDS (to N.Z.)
NIUE (to N.Z.)
Tuamotu Archipelago
Tahiti
FRENCH POLYNESIA
PITCAIRN IS. (to U.K.)
East Pacific Rise
Peru Trench
Callao
Chile Trench
Valparaíso
NEW ZEALAND
Wellington
Southwest Pacific Basin
Pacific-Antarctic Ridge
South East Pacific Basin
C. Horn
EASTERN OCEAN
ANTARCTICA

AUSTRALASIA

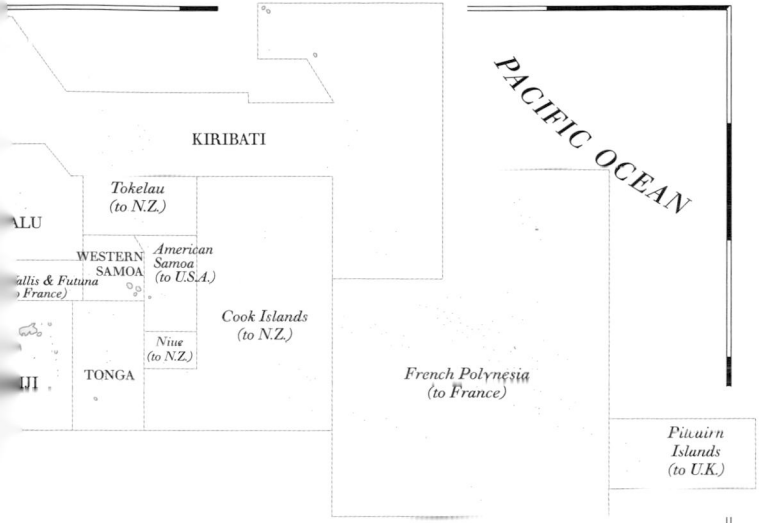

Chatham Island
(to N.Z.)

AUSTRALASIA

Millions of years ago, the continent of Australia and the islands of New Guinea and New Zealand split away from the other southern continents. These island countries have many unique plants and animals, such as Australia's marsupials, or pouched mammals. The thousands of islands scattered in the Pacific are either volcanic islands or coral atolls.

AUSTRALIA AND PAPUA NEW GUINEA

THE SMALLEST, flattest, and driest continent, Australia has a landscape that varies from tropical rainforest to arid desert. Lying to the north, Papua New Guinea (PNG) is so mountainous that its tribes are isolated from each other and from the outside world.

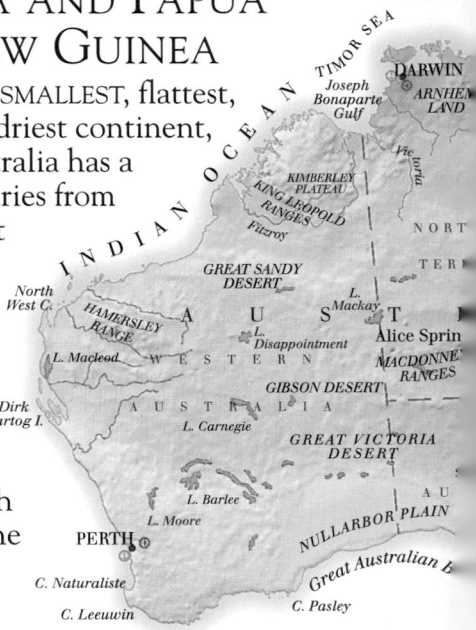

AUSTRALIA
P 18.5 million
L English

CLIMATE

Most people live in temperate zones that occur within 400 km (249 miles) of the coast in the east and southeast, and around Perth in the west. The interior, west, and south are arid; the north is tropical. PNG is tropical, yet snow falls on its highest mountains.

INDUSTRY

Coal, gold, uranium, cattle, tourism, wool, wine- and beer-making Australia is a leading exporter of coal, iron ore, gold, bauxite, and copper, an has the largest known diamond deposi PNG has the largest copper mine in t world and one of the largest gold min

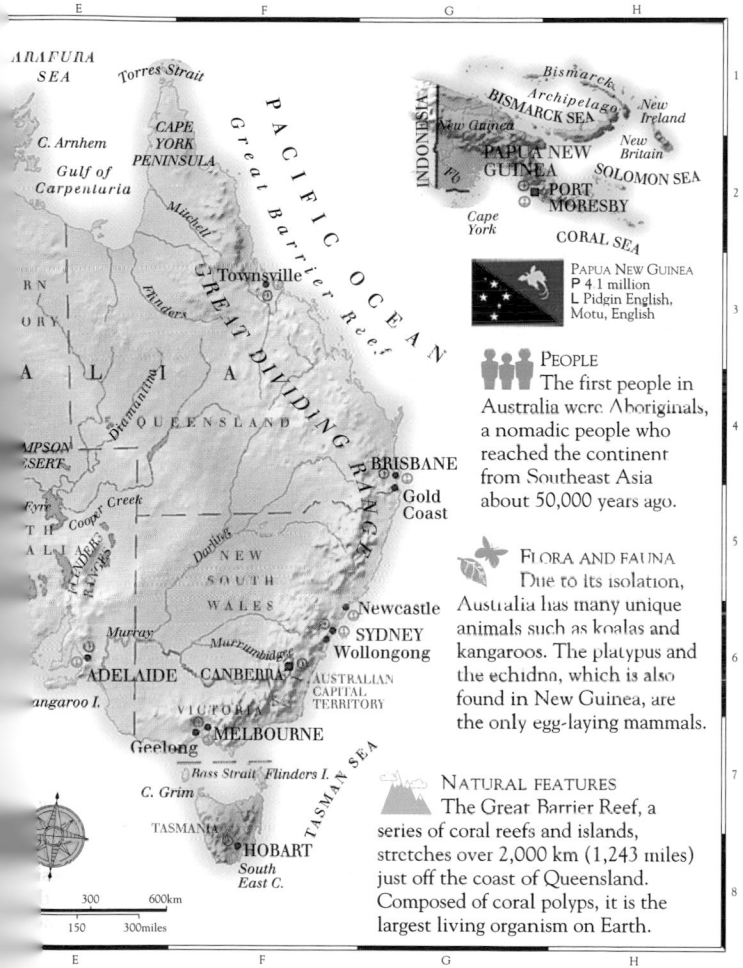

PAPUA NEW GUINEA
P 4.1 million
L Pidgin English, Motu, English

PEOPLE
The first people in Australia were Aboriginals, a nomadic people who reached the continent from Southeast Asia about 50,000 years ago.

FLORA AND FAUNA
Due to its isolation, Australia has many unique animals such as koalas and kangaroos. The platypus and the echidna, which is also found in New Guinea, are the only egg-laying mammals.

NATURAL FEATURES
The Great Barrier Reef, a series of coral reefs and islands, stretches over 2,000 km (1,243 miles) just off the coast of Queensland. Composed of coral polyps, it is the largest living organism on Earth.

NEW ZEALAND

ONE OF THE LAST places on Earth to be inhabited by people, New Zealand lies about halfway between the equator and the South Pole. It is made up of the main North and South Islands, separated by the Cook Strait, and numerous smaller islands. The first settlers were Maoris, who came from the Polynesian islands about 1,200 years ago.

FLORA AND FAUNA
Many of New Zealand's animals have been introduced – two species of bat are the only native land mammals. New

NATURAL FEATURES
New Zealand lies on the "Ring of Fire", a band of volcanic activity that almost encircles the Pacific Ocean. New Zealand has about 400 earthquakes each year, although only about 100 are strong enough to be felt.

PEOPLE
In recent years, Maoris have protested the lack of observance of the Treaty of Waitangi, which protected their rights. About 10 per cent of the total population are Maori.

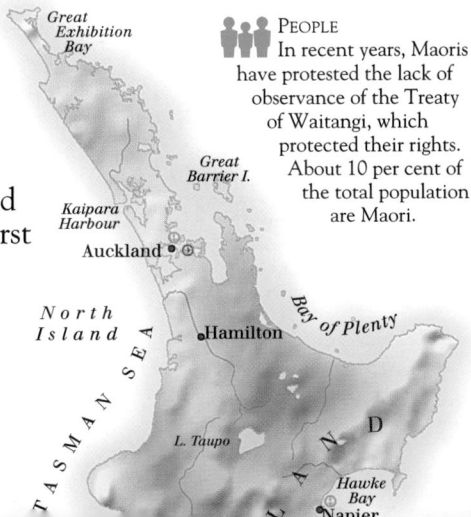

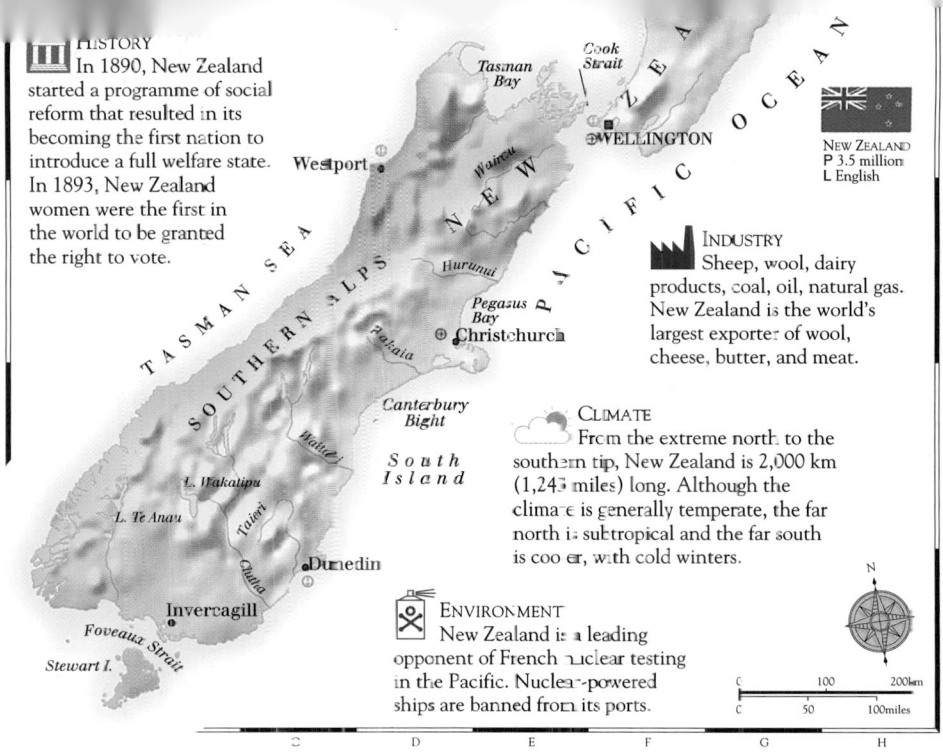

HISTORY

In 1890, New Zealand started a programme of social reform that resulted in its becoming the first nation to introduce a full welfare state. In 1893, New Zealand women were the first in the world to be granted the right to vote.

NEW ZEALAND
P 3.5 million
L English

INDUSTRY

Sheep, wool, dairy products, coal, oil, natural gas. New Zealand is the world's largest exporter of wool, cheese, butter, and meat.

CLIMATE

From the extreme north to the southern tip, New Zealand is 2,000 km (1,243 miles) long. Although the climate is generally temperate, the far north is subtropical and the far south is cooler, with cold winters.

ENVIRONMENT

New Zealand is a leading opponent of French nuclear testing in the Pacific. Nuclear-powered ships are banned from its ports.

Index

Grid references in the Index help find places on the map. If you look up Nairobi in the Index, you will see 96 F4. The first number, 96, is the page number on which the map of Nairobi appears. Next, find the letters and numbers which border the page and trace a line across from the letter and down from the number. This will direct you to the exact grid square in which the city of Nairobi is located.

A

Aachen Germany 67 B5
Ābādān Iran 109 F4
Abakan Rus. Fed. 113 E6
Abeokuta Nigeria 93 F7
Aberdare Range (Mts.) Kenya 96 F4
Aberdeen UK 52 F3/58 G3
Abhā Saudi Arabia 108 D7
Abidjan Ivory Coast 93 E7
Abu Dhabi United Arab Emirates 109 G6
Abu Simbel Egypt 90 C4
Abuja Nigeria 93 F6
Acapulco Mexico 39 F7
Accra Ghana 93 E7
Ad Dammām Saudi Arabia 109 F5
Adana Turkey 105 E6
Adapazari Turkey 104 D4
Addis Ababa Ethiopia 91 E6
Adelaide Australia 133 E6
Aden Yemen 100 C4/109 E8
Aden, Gulf of Arabia/E. Africa 91 G6/100 C4
Adirondack Mts. USA 27 E4
Adriatic Sea S. Europe 72 E4
Aegean Sea Greece/Turkey 79 F4/104 C5
Afghanistan (Country) 110 – 111
Agadir Morocco 88 C3
Agartala India 117 G4
Agra India 117 E3
Ahmadabad India 117 E4
Ahvāz Iran 109 F3
Akron USA 31 H6
Aktyubinsk Kazakhstan 112 C6
Al Āmarāh Iran 109 F3
Al Āqabah Jordan 107 C7
Al Burayqah Libya 89 G4
Al Hufūf Saudi Arabia 109 F5
Al Ḥasakah Syria 106 G3
Al Lādhiqīah Syria 106 D3
Al Mukhā Yemen 108 D8
Al-Basrah Iraq 109 F3
Al-Hillah Iraq 109 E3
Alabama (State) USA 29 E4
Alaska (State) USA 22
Alaska Range (Mts.) USA 22 C4
Alaska, Gulf of USA 22 C5/129 F2
Albania (Country) 77
Albany USA 27 F5
Albert, Lake Uganda/Zaire 95 H5/96 D3
Alberta (Province) Canada 23 E7
Ålborg Denmark 57 B7
Albuquerque USA 35 E4
Aldabra Is. Seychelles 101 C5
Aleutian Is. Alaska USA 22 A4/129 E2
Alexandria Egypt 90 C3
Algeria (Country) 88 – 89
Algiers Algeria 89 E2
Alice Springs Australia 132 D4
Allahabad India 117 F4
Allegheny Mts. USA 29 G2
Allentown USA 27 E6
Almalyk Uzbekistan 111 F3
Alps (Mts.) 63 G5/68 C6/72 C3
Altai Mts. Asia 118 D3
Altun Mts. China 118 C5
Amakusa Sea Japan 123 A6
Amarillo USA 35 F4
Amazon (R.) Brazil/Peru 45 C5/46 D4/53 C5
Ambon Indonesia 127 F7
American Samoa (I.) USA 129 E5
Amiens France 63 E2
Amirante Is. Seychelles 101 D5
Amman Jordan 107 D5
Amritsar India 117 E2
Amsterdam Netherlands 64 D3
Amu Darya (R.) Turkmenistan 111 E4
Amundsen Sea Antarctica 50 B6
Amur (R.) China/Rus. Fed 113 G6/119 G1/120 G1

An Nāṣīryah Iraq 109 F3
An-Najaf Iraq 109 E3
Anadyr' Rus. Fed. 113 H2
Anchorage Alaska USA 22 C5
Andalusia Spain 61 E7
Andaman Is. India 100 F4
Andaman Sea Indian Ocean 104 F4/125 C5
Andes (Mts.) 45–46/48–49
Andizhan Uzbekistan 111 F3
Andorra (Country) 63 E8
Andorra la Vella Andorra 63 E8
Andros (I.) Greece 79 F5
Angarsk Rus. Fed. 113 F6
Angeles Philippines 127 E2
Anglesey (I.) UK 59 E6
Angola (Country) 98
Angren Uzbekistan 111 F3
Anguilla UK 43 H5
Ankara Turkey 105 E4
Ann Arbor USA 31 G5
Annaba Algeria 89 F2
Annapolis USA 29 H2
Anshan China 120 G3
Antakya Turkey 104 D6/105 F6
Antananarivo Madagascar 101 C5
Antarctica (Continent) 50/129 F8
Antigua & Barbuda (Country) 43 H5
Antwerp Netherlands 65 D5
Apeldoorn Netherlands 64 F3
Apennines (Mts.) Italy 72 D4
Appalachian Mts. USA 26 D7/29 F3
Aqaba, Gulf of S.W. Asia 90 D5/107 C7/108 D5
Arabia (Country) 100 C4
Arabian Sea 100 D4/109 G8/116 C4
Arad Romania 76 C3
Arafura Sea Australia 127 G7/128 C5/133 E1
Araguaia (R.) Brazil 47 E5
Arāk Iran 109 F3
Aral Sea Kazakhstan/Uzbekistan 110 D1/112 C6
Arctic Ocean 22 C3/51/56 F2/129 E1
Ardabīl Iran 109 F1
Ardennes (Mts.) Belgium 65 E6
Arequipa Peru 45 C7
Argentina (Country) 48–49
Århus Denmark 57 B7
Arica Chile 48 A2
Arizona (State) USA 34 D4
Arkansas (State) USA 28 C3
Arkhangel'sk Rus. Fed. 82 D4/112 C3
Arlon Belgium 65 F7
Armenia (Country) 85
Arnhem Netherlands 64 F4
Arno (R.) Italy 72 C4
Aruba Netherlands 43 F7
As Sulaymānīyah Iraq 109 F2
Ascension I. UK 53 E6
Ashkhabad Turkmenistan 110 D4
Asmara Eritrea 91 E5
Assen Netherlands 64 F2
Astrakhan Rus. Fed. 83 C7/112 C6
Astana Kazakhstan 112 D6
Asunción Paraguay 48 E3
Aswân Egypt 90 D4
Asyût Egypt 90 C3
Atacama Desert Chile 48 B3
Athens Greece 79 E5
Atlanta USA 29 E4
Atlantic Ocean 46 F3/48–49/51 F8/52–53/62/88/ 92 C7/95 B6/98–99
Atlas Mts. Morocco 88 D3
Attawapiskat Canada 24 D4
Auckland NZ 134 F3
Augsburg Germany 67 F7
Augusta USA 27 G3
Austin USA 35 G6
Australia (Country) 132–133
Australian Capital Territory Australia 133 F6
Austria (Country) 69
Axel Heiberg I. Canada 23 F2/51 F5
Ayutthaya Thailand 125 D5
Az Zarqā Jordan 107 D5
Azerbaijan (Country) 85
Azores (Is.) Portugal 52 E4
Azov, Sea of Rus. Fed./Ukraine 83 A6/85 E5

B
Babruysk Belorussia 81 F6
Bacău Romania 76 F3
Bacolod Philippines 127 E3
Badlands USA 33 E2
Baffin Bay Canada/Greenland 23 F3/51F6/52 C3

Bafoussam Cameroon 95 C5
Baghdad Iraq 109 E3
Baguio Philippines 127 E2
Bahamas (Country) 43 E2
Bahrain (Country) 109 F5
Baia Mare Romania 76 D3
Baikal, Lake Rus. Fed. 113 F6
Baja California Mexico 38 C3
Baker City USA 36 D4
Bakersfield USA 37 D7
Bakhtarān Iran 109 F2
Baku Azerbaijan 85 H7
Balaton, Lake Hungary 75 D7
Balearic Is. Spain 61 H5
Bali (I.) Indonesia 126 D8
Balikesir Turkey 104 C4
Balikpapan Indonesia 126 D6
Balkan Mts. S.E. Europe 77 D5
Balkhash, Lake Kazakhstan 112 D7
Balsas (R.) Mexico 39 F6
Baltic Sea N. Europe 52 G3/70–71 D1/80 B4
Baltimore USA 29 H2
Bamako Mali 92 D5
Ban Me Thuot Vietnam 125 G6
Banda Sea Indonesia 127 F7
Bandar Seri Begawan Brunei 126 D5
Bandar-e Abbās Iran 109 G5
Bandundu Congo (Zaire) 95 D6
Bandung Indonesia 126 C8
Bangalore India 117 E7
Bangkok Thailand 125 D5
Bangladesh (Country) 117 G4
Bangui Central African Republic 95 E5
Banja Luka Bosnia & Herzegovina 75 E6
Banjarmasin Indonesia 126 D7
Banjul Gambia 92 B5
Banská Bystrica Slovakia 71 E7
Baotou China 119 F4
Baranavichy Belorussia 81 D6
Barbados (Country) 43 H7
Barcelona Spain 61 G3
Bareilly India 111 F3
Barents Sea Arctic Ocean 51 H6/82 E3/112 D3
Bari Italy 73 G5
Barinas Venezuela 44 C3
Barnaul Rus. Fed. 113 E6
Barquisimeto Venezuela 44 D3
Barranquilla Colombia 44 B3
Barysaw Belorussia 81 F6
Basle Switzerland 68 B4
Basque Provinces Spain 61 E2
Bassein Burma 125 B5
Bata Equatorial Guinea 95 B5
Batangas Philippines 127 E2
Bătdâmbâng Cambodia 125 E6
Baton Rouge USA 28 D5
Bavaria Germany 67 F6
Bavarian Alps (Mts.) Germany 67 F7
Bayan Har Mts. China 118 D6
Beaufort Sea 22 D3/51 F3
Beaumont USA 35 H6
Béchar Algeria 88 D3
Beersheba Israel 107 C6
Beira Mozambique 99 G5/101 B6
Beirut Lebanon 106 C4
Beja Portugal 60 C6
Belém Brazil 46 F4
Belfast Northern Ireland UK 59 D5
Belgium (Country) 65
Belgrade Yugoslavia 76 B4
Belize (Country) 42 B4
Bellevue USA 36 B3
Bellingshausen Sea Antarctica 50 B4
Belmopan Belize 42 B4
Belo Horizonte Brazil 47 F6
Belorussia (Country) 81
Bengal, Bay of India/South Asia 100 F4/117 G5/124 A4
Benghazi Libya 89 G3
Benin (Country) 93 F6
Berbera Somalia 91 G6
Berbérati Central African Republic 95 D5
Bergen Norway 52 F3/57 A5
Bergen op Zoom Netherlands 64 C4
Bering Sea Pacific Ocean 22 B4/113 H2/129 E2
Bering Strait Arctic Ocean/Pacific Ocean 22 B3/113 H1/129 E1
Berlin Germany 66 G4
Bermuda (I.) UK 52 C4
Bern Switzerland 68 B4
Bernese Alps (Mts.) Switzerland 68 B6
Beskid Mts. Poland 71 F
Bhopal India 117 E4

Bhutan (Country) 117 G3
Bielefeld Germany 66 D4
Bien Hoa Vietnam 125 G6
Bila Tserkva Ukraine 84 D3
Birmingham UK 59 F6
Birmingham USA 29 E4
Biscay, Bay of Spain 61 E1
Bishkek Kyrgyzstan 111 G2
Bissau Guinea-Bissau 92 C4
Bitola Macedonia 77 C6
Biysk Rus. Fed. 113 E6
Black (R.) China/Vietnam 124 E4
Black Forest Germany 67 D6
Black Sea 77 H6/83 A7/85 G6/104 – 105
Blagoveshchensk Rus. Fed. 113 G6
Blanco, Cape USA 36 A4
Blantyre Malawi 97 F7
Bob-Dioulasso Burkina 93 E6
Bogor Indonesia 126 C7
Bogotá Colombia 44 B4
Bohemia Czech Republic 70 C6
Boise USA 32 C3
Bolivia (Country) 45 E7
Bologna Italy 72 D4
Bombay India 100 E4/117 E5
Bomu (R.) Central African Republic/Congo (Zaire) 95 F5
Bonifacio, Strait of Sardinia 73 B5
Bonn Germany 67 C5
Borås Sweden 57 C7
Bordeaux France 62 D6
Borneo (I.) Indonesia 101 G5/126 D5
Bosnia & Herzegovina (Country) 74 – 75
Bosporus Turkey 104 D3
Boston USA 27 G5
Bothnia, Gulf of Sweden/Finland 57 E5
Botswana (Country) 99
Bouvet I. Norway 53 F7
Bradford UK 59 G5
Brahmaputra (var. Yarlung Zangbo) (R.) 117 H3/118 C7
Brăila Romania 76 G4
Brasília Brazil 47 F5
Braşov Romania 76 E4
Bratislava Slovakia 70 D7
Brazil (Country) 46 – 47
Brazilian Highlands (Mts.) Brazil 47 G5
Brazzaville Congo 95 D6
Brecon Beacons (Mts.) UK 59 E7
Breda Netherlands 64 D4
Bregenz Austria 68 D4
Bremen Germany 66 D3
Brest Belorussia 81 C7
Brest France 62 C3
Bridgeport USA 27 F6
Brisbane Australia 133 G4
Bristol UK 59 F7
Bristol Bay Alaska USA 22 B5
British Columbia (Province) Canada 22 D7
British Indian Ocean Territory UK 101 E5
British Virgin Is. UK 43 H5
Brittany France 62 C3
Brno Czech Republic 70 D6
Bruges Belgium 65 B5
Brunei (Country) 126 D4
Brunswick Germany 66 E4
Brussels Belgium 65 D5
Bucharest Romania 76 E4
Budapest Hungary 75 E2
Buenaventura Colombia 44 B4
Buenos Aires Argentina 49 E5/53 C6
Buenos Aires, Lake Argentina 49 C7
Buffalo USA 26 D4
Bug (R.) Poland/Ukraine 71 F3
Bujumbura Burundi 96 D4
Bukavu Congo (Zaire) 95 G6
Bukhara Uzbekistan 111 E4
Bulawayo Zimbabwe 99 E5
Bulgaria (Country) 77
Buraydah Saudi Arabia 109 E4
Burgas Bulgaria 77 F5
Burgundy France 63 F3
Burkina (Country) 93 E5
Burma (Country) 124
Bursa Turkey 104 D4
Buru (I.) Indonesia 127 F6
Burundi (Country) 96 D4
Butuan Philippines 127 F3
Buzău Romania 76 F4
Bydgoszcz Poland 71 E3

C

Cabanatuan Philippines 127 E2
Cabinda Angola 98 A3
Cabora Bassa, Lake Mozambique 98 F4
Cadiz Philippines 127 E3
Caen France 62 D2
Caesarea Israel 107 C5
Cagayan de Oro Philippines 127 F4

Cagliari Sardinia 73 B6
Cairo Egypt 90 C3
Calabria Italy 73 G6
Calais France 63 E1
Calbayog Philippines 127 F3
Calcutta India 100 F3/117 G4
Calgary Canada 23 E8
Cali Colombia 44 B4
California (State) USA 37 C7
Callao Peru 45 B6/129 H5
Cambodia (Country) 125
Cambrian Mts. UK 59 E6
Cameroon (Country) 95
Campeche Mexico 39 H6
Campinas Brazil 47 F6
Can Tho Vietnam 125 F6
Canaveral, Cape USA 29 F7
Canberra Australia 133 F6
Caniapiscau, Lake Canada 25 E4
Canton China 121 E5
Cape Town South Africa 53 G6/99 C7/101 B6
Capeenda Camulemba Angola 98 C3
Cappadocia Turkey 105 F5
Capri (I.) Italy 73 E6
Caracas Venezuela 44 D3
Cardiff UK 59 E7
Caribbean Sea 44 C2/53 B5
Carpathians (Mts.) E. Europe 71 E6/76
Carpentaria, Gulf of Australia E2 133
Carson City USA 34 C2
Cartagena Colombia 44 B3
Casablanca Morocco 88 D3
Casper USA 33 E4
Caspian Sea Asia/Europe 83 C7/85 H7/109 G1/112 B6
Catalonia Spain 61 G3
Catania Sicily 73 F7
Catskill Mts. USA 27 E5
Caucasus (Mts.) 83 B7/85 F6
Cayenne French Guiana 44 H4
Cedar Rapids USA 33 H4
Celebes (I.) Indonesia 127 E6
Central African Republic (Country) 95 E5
Cephalonia (I.) Greece 78 D4
Cevennes (Mts.) France 63 F7
Chad (Country) 94 E3
Chad, Lake C. Africa 93 H5/94 D4
Chagai Hills Pakistan 116 C2
Chalbi Desert Kenya 96 G3
Changchun China 120 G2
Changsha China 121 E5
Channel Is. UK 59 F8/62 C2
Chardzhou Turkmenistan 111 E4
Charleroi Belgium 65 D6
Charleston (South Carolina) USA 29 F5
Charleston (West Virginia) USA 29 F2
Charlottetown Canada 25 F6
Chattanooga USA 29 E3
Cheju South Korea 120 G4
Chelyabinsk Rus. Fed. 112 D5
Chemnitz Germany 67 G5
Chengdu China 120 C4
Cherbourg France 62 D2
Chernihiv Ukraine 84 D2
Chernivtsi Ukraine 84 C4
Chernobyl Ukraine 84 D2
Chesapeake Bay USA 29 H2
Cheyenne USA 33 E4
Chiang Mai Thailand 124 D4
Chiba Japan 123 F5
Chicago USA 31 F5
Chiclayo Peru 45 A6
Chico USA 37 B6
Chidley, Cape Canada 25 F2
Chihuahua Mexico 39 E3
Chile (Country) 48 – 49
Chillán Chile 49 B5
Chimbote Peru 45 A6
China (Country) 118–121
Chingola Zambia 97 C6
Chios (I.) Greece 79 G3
Chirchik Uzbekistan 111 F3
Chisinau Moldavia 84 D4
Chittagong Bangladesh 117 G4
Chitungwiza Zimbabwe 99 F5
Chon Buri Thailand 125 D6
Ch'ŏngjin North Korea 120 H2
Christchurch NZ 135 D6
Christmas I. Australia G5 101
Chukchi Sea Arctic Ocean 51 G2
Chungking China 120 C4
Churchill Canada 23 F6
Churchill (R.) Canada

23 F7
Cincinnati USA 31 G7
Cirebon Indonesia 126 C8
Ciudad Bolívar Venezuela 44 E3
Ciudad del Este Argentina 48 F3
Ciudad Guayana Venezuela 44 E3
Ciudad Juárez Mexico 39 E2
Ciudad Madero Mexico 39 F5
Clermont-Ferrand France 63 E5
Cleveland USA 31 H5
Cluj-Napoca Romania 76 C3
Coatzacoalcos Mexico 39 G7
Cochabamba Bolivia 45 D7
Cochin India 100 E4/117 E7
Cod, Cape USA 27 G5
Coeur d'Alene USA 32 C2
Coihaique Chile 49 C7
Coimbatore India 117 E7
Coimbra Portugal 60 C4
Cologne Germany 67 C5
Colombia (Country) 44 C4
Colombo Sri Lanka 117 F8
Colorado (R.) USA 34 D4/129 G3
Colorado (State) USA 35 F3
Colorado Springs USA 35 F3
Columbia (R.) USA 36 C3
Columbia (South Carolina) USA 29 F4
Columbus (Georgia) USA 29 E4
Como, Lake Italy 72 C3
Comodoro Rivadavia Argentina 49 C7
Comoros (Country) 101 C5
Conakry Guinea 92 C6
Concepción Chile 49 B6
Concord USA 27 F4/37 B6
Congo (Country) 95 D6
Congo (R.) Congo (Zaire) 95 E5
Connecticut (R.) USA 27 F4
Connecticut (State) USA 27 F5
Constance, Lake Switzerland 67 D7/68 C4
Constanța Romania 76 G4
Constantine Algeria 89 F2
Cook Is. New Zealand 129 E5
Copenhagen Denmark 57 B7
Copiapó Chile 48 B4
Coquimbo Chile 48 B4
Coral Sea Pacific Ocean 128 D5/133 H2
Córdoba Argentina 48 C4
Corfu Greece 78 C3
Corinth, Gulf of Greece 79 E5
Cork Ireland 59 B6
Corpus Christi USA 35 G7
Corrientes Argentina 48 E4
Costa Rica (Country) 42 C7
Côte d'Azur France 63 G7
Craiova Romania 76 D4
Crete Greece 79 F8
Crete, Sea of Greece 79 F7
Crimea Rus. Fed./Ukraine 85 E5
Croatia (Country) 74–75
Cubango (R.) Southern Africa 98 B4
Culiacán Mexico 39 D4
Cumaná Venezuela 44 E3
Curitiba Brazil 47 E7
Cyclades (Is.) 79 F6
Cyprus (Country) 105
Czech Republic (Country) 70–71

D

Da Lat Vietnam 125 G6
Da Nang Vietnam 125 G5
Dacca Bangladesh 117 G4
Dagupan Philippines 127 E2
Dakar Senegal 92 B5
Dakhla Western Sahara 88 B5
Dalian China 120 F3
Dallas USA 35 G5
Damascus Syria 106 D4
Danube (R.) C. Europe 67 E7/69 G2/71 E6/74 E2/77 C4
Dar es Salaam Tanzania 97 G5/101 C5
Darling (R.) Australia 133 F5
Darwin Australia 132 D1
Datong China 120 E3
Daugavpils Latvia 81 E5
Davao Philippines 127 F4
Davis Sea Antarctica 50 D5
Davis Strait Greenland/Canada 23 G3/51 E7
Dawson Canada 22 D5
Dayton USA 31 G7
Dead Sea Israel 107 C5
Death Valley USA 37 E7
Debrecen Hungary 75 G2
Delaware (State) USA 27 E7
Denmark (Country) 56
Denmark Strait 51 F8
Denpasar Indonesia

126 D8
Denver USA 35 F2
Derby UK 59 G6
Des Moines USA 33 G4
Detroit USA 31 G5
Devon I. Canada 23 F3/51 F5
Dezfūl Iran 109 F3
Dhanbad India 117 G4
Dharwad India 117 E6
Dieppe France 63 E2
Dijon France 63 F4
Dinaric Alps (Mts.) Bosnia & Herzegovina/Croatia 75 D6
Dire Dawa Ethiopia 91 F6
Diyarbakir Turkey 105 G5
Djibouti (Country) 91
Djibouti Djibouti 91 F6/100 C4
Dnieper (R.) E. Europe 81 G7/83 B5/85 E4
Dniester (R.) Ukraine/Moldavia 84 C3
Dnipropetrovs'k Ukraine 85 E4
Dobrich Bulgaria 77 F5
Dodecanese (Is.) Greece 79 G6
Dodoma Tanzania 97 F5
Doha Qatar 109 F5
Dolomites (Mts.) Italy 72 D3
Dominica (Country) 43 H6
Dominican Republic (Country) 43 F4
Don (R.) Rus. Fed. 83 B6
Donets (R.) Rus. Fed./Ukraine 85 E3
Donets'k Ukraine 85 F4
Dongguang China 121 E5
Dordogne (R.) France 63 E6
Dordrecht Netherlands 64 D4
Dortmund Germany 66 C4
Douala Cameroon 95 B5
Dover USA 27 E7
Dover, Strait of France/UK 63 E1
Drakensberg (Mts.) South Africa 99 E7
Dresden Germany 67 H5
Drin (R.) Albania 77 B5
Drobeta-Turnu-Severin Romania 76 C4
Dubai United Arab Emirates 109 G5
Dublin Ireland 59 D5
Dubrovnik Croatia 75 E8
Duero (R.) Spain 61 E3
Duisberg Germany 66 C4
Dunedin NZ 135 C8
Durance (R.) France 63 G7
Durban South Africa 99 F7/101 B6
Durham USA 29 G3
Dushanbe Tajikistan 111 F4
Düsseldorf Germany 67 C5
Dvina, Western (R.) Belorussia 81 F5
Dzhizak Uzbekistan 111 E3
Dzhugdzhur Range (Mts.) Rus. Fed. 113 G5

E

East China Sea 120 G4/123 A7
East London South Africa 99 E7
East Siberian Sea Arctic Ocean 51 H3/113 G2
Ebro (R.) Spain 61 F3
Ecuador (Country) 45 A5
Edinburgh UK 59 F4
Edmonton Canada 23 E7
Edward, Lake Uganda/Congo (Zaire) 95–96
Edwards Plateau USA 35 G6
Egypt (Country) 90 C4
Eindhoven Netherlands 64 E4
Eisenstadt Austria 69 H3
El Aaiun Western Sahara 88 C4
El Faiyûm Egypt 90 C3
El Mansûra Egypt 90 C3
El Minya Egypt 90 C3
El Obeid Sudan 91 C6
El Paso USA 35 E6
El Salvador (Country) 42 B5
Elat Israel 107 C6
Elăziğ Turkey 105 G5
Elba (I.) Italy 73 C5
Elbe (R.) Germany 66 F3
Elburz Mts. Iran 109 G2
Ellesmere I. Canada 23 F2/51 F5
Ellsworth Mts. Antarctica 50 B5
Ems (R.) Germany 66 C4
En Gedi Israel 107 C5
Enderby Land Antarctica 50 D4
England (Country) 58–59
English Channel France/UK 59/62
Enschede Netherlands 64 G3
Ephesus Turkey 104 C5
Equatorial Guinea (Country) 95 C5
Erfurt Germany 67 F5
Erie, Lake Canada/USA 24 D8/26 D5/31 H5
Eritrea (Country) 91
Erzurum Turkey 105 G3

Eşfāhān Iran 109 G3
Eskişehir Turkey 104 D4
Essen Germany 66 C4
Estonia (Country) 80 D3
Ethiopia (Country) 91
Ethiopian Highlands (Mts.) Ethiopia 91 E6
Eugene USA 36 B4
Euphrates (R.) S.W. Asia 105 F6/106 G3/109 E3
Eureka USA 37 A5
Evansville USA 31 F8
Everett USA 36 B2
Everglades, The USA 29 F8
Evvoia Greece 79 E4
Eyre, Lake Australia 133 E5

F

Faeroe Is. Denmark 52 E3
Fairbanks Alaska USA 22 C4
Faisalabad Pakistan 117 E2
Falkland Is. UK 53 C7
Famagusta Cyprus 105 E7
Farewell, Cape Greenland 52 D3
Fargo USA 33 G2
Faro Portugal 60 C7
Farvel, Cape Greenland 51 E8
Fergana Uzbekistan 111 F3
Fez Morocco 88 D3
Fiji (Country) 129 E5
Finland (Country) 56 – 57
Finland, Gulf of Baltic Sea 57 F6/80 D2
Flinders Ranges (Mts.) Australia 133 E5
Flint USA 31 G5
Florence Italy 72 D4
Flores (I.) Indonesia 127 E8
Florida (State) USA 29 F6
Florida Keys USA 29 F8
Focşani Romania 76 F4
Formosa Paraguay 48 E3
Fort McMurray Canada 23 E7
Fort Wayne USA 31 G6
Fort Worth USA 35 G5
Fortaleza Brazil 46 H4
Forth (R.) UK 58 E4
France (Country) 62 – 63
Francistown Botswana 99 E5
Frankfort USA 29 F2
Frankfurt Germany 67 D5
Frankivs'k Ukraine 84 C3
Franz Josef Land (Is.) Rus. Fed. 51 H6
Fredericton Canada 25 F7
Freetown Sierra Leone 92 C6
Fremantle Australia 101 G6
French Guiana France 44 H4
French Polynesia France 129 F5
Fresno USA 37 C7
Fukuoka Japan 123 B6
Fushun China 120 G3
Fuzhou China 121 F5

G

Gabon (Country) 95 C6
Gaborone Botswana 99 E6
Galápagos Is. Ecuador 129 G4
Galaţi Romania 76 F4
Galicia Poland 71 F6
Galicia Spain 60 D2
Galle Sri Lanka 117 F8
Gallipoli Turkey 104 C4
Galway Ireland 59 B5
Gambia (Country) 92 C5
Gäncä Azerbaijan 85 G7
Gangdise Range (Mts.) China 118 C7
Ganges (R.) India 100 F3/117 F3
Garda, Lake Italy 72 C3
Garonne (R.) France 62 D6
Garoua Cameroon 94 C4
Gary USA 31 F6
Gaza Gaza Strip 107 C5
Gaza Strip 107 C5
Gaziantep Turkey 105 F6
Gdańsk Poland 71 E2
Geelong Australia 133 F7
General Santos Philippines 127 F4
Geneva Switzerland 68 A7
Geneva, Lake France/Switzerland 63 G4/68 B6
Genoa Italy 72 B4
Genoa, Gulf of Italy 72 C4
Georgetown Cayman Is. 42 D4
Georgetown Guyana 44 F3
Georgia (Country) 85
Georgia (State) USA 29 F5
Germany (Country) 66–67
Ghana West Africa 93 E6
Ghāt Libya 89 F5
Ghent Netherlands 65 C5
Gibraltar Gibraltar 60 D8
Gibraltar UK 52 F4/60 D8
Gibraltar, Strait of Morocco/Spain 60 D8/88 D2
Gibson Desert Australia 132 D4
Giza Egypt 90 C3
Glasgow UK 58 E4

Glendale USA 37 D8
Gobi Desert Mongolia 119 E4
Godhavn Greenland 51 F7
Godoy Cruz Argentina 49 B5
Godthåb Greenland 51 E7
Goiânia Brazil 47 E6
Golan Heights 107 D5
Gold Coast Australia 133 G5
Gonder Ethiopia 91 E6
Good Hope, Cape of South Africa 53 G7/99 C7/101 B6
Goosebay Canada 25 F4
Göreme Turkey 105 E5
Gostivar Macedonia 77 C6
Gothenburg Sweden 57 B7
Gozo (I.) Malta 73 F8
Grampian Mts. UK 58 F3
Gran Chaco Argentina 48 C3
Grenada (Country) 43 H8
Grand Canyon USA 34 D3
Grand Rapids USA 31 F5
Grand Turk Turks and Caicos Is. UK 43 F4
Graz Austria 69 G4
Great Barrier I. NZ 134 F3
Great Barrier Reef Australia 128 D5/133 F2
Great Basin USA 34 D1
Great Bear Lake Canada 23 E5
Great Dividing Range (Mts.) Australia 133 F4
Great Plains USA 33 E3
Great Rift Valley E. Africa 96 – 97
Great Salt Lake USA 34 D1
Great Sandy Desert Australia 132 C3
Great Slave Lake Canada 23 E6
Great Victoria Desert Australia 132 D5
Great Wall China 119 E5/120 B3/D3
Greater Antilles 43 E4
Greater Khinghan Range (Mts.) China 119 G3
Greece (Country) 78 – 79
Green Bay USA 31 F4
Greenland Denmark 51/52 D3
Greenland Sea 51 G7/52 F3
Groningen Netherlands 64 G2
Grozny Rus. Fed. 112 B6
Guadalajara Mexico 39 E6
Guadeloupe France 43 H6
Guam (I.) USA 128 D4
Guatemala (Country) 42 B4
Guatemala City Guatemala 42 B4
Guaviare (R.) Colombia/Venezuela 44 C4
Guayaquil Ecuador 45 A5
Guernsey (I.) UK 59 E8
Guinea (Country) 92 C6
Guinea, Gulf of West Africa 95 B5
Guinea-Bissau (Country) 92 C5
Guiyang China 121 C5
Gujranwala Pakistan 117 E2
Guwahati India 117 G3
Guyana (Country) 44 F4
Gwalior India 117 E3
Gyda Peninsula Rus. Fed. 113 E4
Gyumri Armenia 85 G7

H

Haarlem Netherlands 64 D3
Hague, The Netherlands 64 C3
Hai Phong Vietnam 124 F4
Haifa Israel 107 C5
Haikou China 121 D6
Hainan (I.) China 121 D6
Haiti (Country) 43 F4
Ḥalab Syria 106 E3
Halifax Canada 25 F7
Halmahera (I.) Indonesia 127 F5
Hälsingborg Sweden 57 C7
Hamada Japan 123 B5
Ḥamāh Syria 106 D3
Hamburg Germany 66 E3
Hamersley Range (Mts.) Australia 132 B4
Hamilton Canada 24 D8
Hamilton NZ 134 F3
Hammerfest Norway 56 F2
Handan China 120 E3
Hangayn Mts. Mongolia 119 E3
Hangzhou China 120 F4
Hanoi Vietnam 124 F4
Hanover Germany 66 E4
Harare Zimbabwe 99 F5
Harbin China 120 G2
Hardanger Fjord Norway 57 A6
Hargeysa Somalia 91 F6
Harrisburg USA 27 E6
Hartford USA 27 F5
Hat Yai Thailand 125 D7
Havana Cuba 42 D2
Hawaii (Is.) USA 129 E3
Hefei China 120 F4

Hejaz Saudi Arabia 108 D4
Helena USA 32 D2
Helsinki Finland 57 F6
Helwân Egypt 90 C3
Henzada Burma 124 B4
Herāt Afghanistan 110 D6
Hermosillo Mexico 38 D2
Hidaka Mts. Japan 122 F2
Highlands (Mts.) UK 58 E3
Himalayas (Mts.) S. Asia 117 F2/118 C7
Ḥimṣ Syria 106 D4
Hindu Kush (Mts.) Afghanistan 111 F5
Hiroshima Japan 123 B5
Ho Chi Minh City Vietnam 125 F6
Hobart Australia 133 F8
Hodeida Yemen 108 D8
Hohe Tauern (Mts.) Austria 69 F4
Hohhot China 119 F4
Hokkaidō (I.) Japan 122 F2
Holon Israel 107 C5
Homyel' Belorussia 81 G7
Honduras (Country) 42 B4
Hong Gai Vietnam 124 G4
Hong Kong 121 E6/ 128 C3
Hongshui He (R.) China 121 C5
Honolulu USA 129 E3
Honshū (I.) Japan 122 E4
Horlivka Ukraine 85 F4
Hormuz, Strait of Iran/ Oman 109 G5
Horn of Africa Somalia 91 H6
Horn, Cape Chile 49 D8/ 53 C7/129 H7
Houston USA 35 H6
Hrodna Belorussia 81 C6
Huainan China 120 E4
Huambo Angola 98 B4
Huancayo Peru 45 B6
Hudson Bay Canada 24 D3/23 G5
Hudson Strait Canada 23 G4/25 E1
Hue Vietnam 125 G5
Hulun Nur (Lake) China 119 G2
Hungary (Country) 74–76
Huntsville USA 29 E3
Huron, Lake Canada/USA 24 C7/31 G3
Hyderabad India 117 E6
Hyderabad Pakistan 116 D3

I
Iaşi Romania 76 F3
Ibadan Nigeria 93 F7
Ibiza Balearic Is. Spain 61 G5
Ica Peru 45 B7
Iceland (Country) 52 E3
Idaho (State) USA 32 C3
Īlām Iran 109 F3
Ilebo Zaire 95 E6
Iligan Philippines 127 F4
Illinois (R.) USA 31 E7
Illinois (State) USA 31 E6
Iloilo Philippines 127 E3
Ilorin Nigeria 93 F6
Imphal India 117 H4
Inch'ŏn South Korea 120 G3
India (Country) 116–117
Indian Ocean 91 H7/ 99–101/126 C8
Indiana (State) USA F6
Indianapolis USA 31 F7
Indigirka (R.) Rus. Fed. 113 G3
Indonesia (Country) 126–127
Indore India 117 E4
Indus (R.) Pakistan 116 D3
Inn (R.) Austria 69 E4
Inner Mongolia China 119 G3
Innsbruck Austria 69 E5
Insein Burma 125 C5
Invercargill NZ 135 B8
Ionian Is. Greece 78 C4
Ionian Sea Greece 73 H7/ 78 C4
Ios (I.) Greece 79 F6
Iowa (State) USA 33 G4
Ipoh Malaysia 125 D8
Iquitos Peru 45 C5
Iraklion Greece 79 F8
Iran (Country) 109 G3
Iraq (Country) 109 E2
Irbid Jordan 107 D5
Irbil Iraq 109 F2
Ireland (Country) 58–59
Irian Jaya Indonesia 127 H6
Irish Sea 59
Irkutsk Rus. Fed. 113 F6
Irrawaddy (R.) Burma 24 C3/100 F3
Ishikari Mts. Japan 122 F2
Islamabad Pakistan 117 E1
Ismā'īlīya Egypt 90 D3
Isparta Turkey 104 D5
Israel (Country) 107
Istanbul Turkey 104 D4
Italy (Country) 72–73
Ivory Coast (Country) 92 D7
Izhevsk Rus. Fed. 83 E5/ 112 C5
Izmir Turkey 104 C5

Izmit Turkey 104 D3

J

Jabalpur India 117 F4
Jackson USA 28 D4
Jacksonville USA 29 F6
Jaffna Sri Lanka 117 F7
Jaipur India 117 E3
Jakarta Indonesia 126 C7
Jalandhar India 117 E2
Jamaica (Country) 43 E4
Jambi Indonesia 126 B6
James Bay Canada 24 D4
Jan Mayen I. Norway 51 G8
Japan (Country) 122–123
Japan, Sea of E. Asia 113 H6/122 D4/128 D2
Java (I.) Indonesia 101 G5/126 C8
Java Sea Indonesia 126 C7
Jayapura Indonesia 127 H6
Jedda Saudi Arabia 108 D5
Jefferson City USA 33 H5
Jember Indonesia 126 D8
Jersey (I.) UK 59 F8
Jerusalem Israel 107 C5
Jilin China 120 G2
Jinan China 120 E3
Jingdezhen China 120 F5
Jodhpur India 117 E3
Johannesburg South Africa 99 E6
Johor Baharu Malaysia 125 E8
Jönköping Sweden 57 C7
Jordan (Country) 107
Juan de Fuca, Strait of USA/Canada 36 A2
Juneau Alaska 22 D6
Jutland Denmark 57 A7

K

Kabul Afghanistan 111 F6
Kabwe Kenya 97 C7
Kagoshima Japan 123 B6
Kahramanmaraş Turkey 105 F5
Kalahari Desert Botswana 99 D6
Kalemie Congo (Zaire) 95 G7
Kaliningrad Rus. Fed. 81 B5
Kamchatka Rus. Fed. 113 H3
Kampala Uganda 96 E3
Kâmpóng Cham Cambodia 125 F6
Kananga Congo (Zaire) 95 F7
Kano Nigeria 93 G5
Kanpur India 117 F3
Kansas (State) USA 33 G5
Kansas City USA 33 G5
Kao-hsiung Taiwan 121 F5
Kara Sea Rus. Fed. 51 H5/82 G3/112 D3
Karachi Pakistan 100 E3/116 D3
Karaganda Kazakhstan 112 D6
Karakorum Mts. China 118 B5
Karakum Canal Turkmenistan 110 C4
Karbala Iraq 109 E3
Kariba, Lake Zambia/Congo (Zaire) 97 C7/99 E5
Karlsruhe Germany 67 D6
Karpathos (I.) Greece 79 G7
Karshi Uzbekistan 111 E4
Kasai (R.) Congo (Zaire) 95 E6
Kathmandu Nepal 117 F3
Katowice Poland 71 E6
Kattegat Denmark 57 B7
Kaunas Lithuania 81 C5
Kawasaki Japan 123 F5
Kayseri Turkey 105 E5
Kazakhstan (Country) 112
Kazan' Rus. Fed. 83 D6/112 C5
Kediri Indonesia 126 D8
Kelang Malaysia 125 D8
Kendari Indonesia 127 E6
Kentucky (State) USA 29 E2
Kenya (Country) 96
Kermān Iran 109 G4
Khabarovsk Rus. Fed. 113 H6
Khadzhent Tajikistan 111 F3
Kharkiv Ukraine 85 E3
Khartoum Sudan 91 D5
Khasab Oman 109 G5
Kherson Ukraine 85 E4
Khmel'nyts'kyy Ukraine 84 D3
Khon Kaen Thailand 125 E5
Khulna Bangladesh 117 G4
Khyber Pass Afghanistan/Pakistan 111 F6
Kiel Germany 66 E2
Kiev Ukraine 84 D3
Kigali Rwanda 96 D4
Kikwit Congo (Zaire) 95 E7
Kimberley South Africa 99 D7
King Leopold Range (Mts.) Australia 132 C3
Kingston Jamaica 43 E4
Kinshasa Congo (Zaire) 95 D6
Kirghiz Range (Mts.) Kyrgyzstan 111 G2
Kiribati (Country) 129 E4
Kirkūk Iraq 109 F2
Kirov Rus. Fed. 112 C4
Kisangani Congo (Zaire) 95 F6

Kismaayo Somalia 91 F8
Kitakyūhū Japan 123 B6
Kithira (I.) Greece 79 E7
Kivu, Lake Congo (Zaire) 95 G6
Kizilirmak (R.) Turkey 105 E4
Kjølen (Mts.) Norway 56 D4
Klagenfurt Austria 69 G5
Klaipéda Lithuania 81 B5
Klamath Falls USA 37 C5
Klerksdorp South Africa 99 E6
Knud Rasmussen Land Greenland 51 F6
Kōbe Japan 123 D5/128 D3
Kokand Uzbekistan 111 F3
Kola Peninsula Rus. Fed. 82 D3
Kolyma (R.) Rus. Fed. 113 G3
Konya Turkey 105 E5
Korea Strait Korea/Japan 120 H5/123 A5
Kos (I.) Greece 79 G6
Košice Slovakia 71 F7
Kosovska Mitrovica Yugoslavia 77 B5
Kota Baharu Malaysia 125 E7
Kota India 117 E5
Kota Kinabalu Malaysia 126 D4
Kowloon Hong Kong 121 E6
Kraków Poland 71 E6
Kraljevo Yugoslavia 76 B4
Kramators'k Ukraine 85 E4
Krasnodar Rus. Fed. 83 A7/112 B5
Krasnovodsk Turkmenistan 110 B3
Krasnoyarsk Rus. Fed. 113 E6
Kruševac Yugoslavia 76 C4
Kryvyy Rih Ukraine 85 E4
Kuala Lumpur Malaysia 125 E8
Kuantan Malaysia 125 E8
Kuching Malaysia 126 C5
Kumamoto Japan 123 B6
Kumanovo Macedonia 77 C5
Kumasi Ghana 93 E7
Kunlun Mts. China 118 C6
Kunming China 121 B5
Kupa (R.) Croatia 74 D5
Kupang Indonesia 127 F8
Kurile Is. E. Asia/Rus. Fed. 113 H5/122 G1/128 D2
Kuşadasi Turkey 104 C5
Kustanai Kazakhstan 112 D6
Kütahya Turkey 104 D4
K'ut'aisi Georgia 85 G6
Kuujjuaq Canada 25 E2
Kuwait (Country) 109 F4
Kuwait City Kuwait 109 F4
Kwilu (R.) Angola/Congo (Zaire) 95 E7
Kyaikkami Burma 125 C5
Kyōto Japan 123 D5
Kyrgyzstan (Country) 111
Kyūshu (I.) Japan 123 B6
Kyzyl Rus. Fed. 113 E6
Kzyl-Orda Kazakhstan 112 D7

L

La Guaira Venezuela 53 C5
La Paz Bolivia 45 D7
La Paz Mexico 38 D4
La Pérouse Strait Japan 122 E1
La Serena Chile 48 B4
Labrador (Province) Canada 25 F4
Labrador Sea 25 F2/52 C3
Ladoga, Lake Rus. Fed. 82 C4
Lagos Nigeria 52 F5/93 F7
Lagos Portugal 60 C7
Lahore Pakistan 117 E2
Lake District UK 59 F5
Lakshadweep Is. India 101 E4
Lansing USA 31 G5
Lanzhou China 120 C3
Laos (Country) 124–125
Laptev Sea Rus. Fed. 51 H4/113 F3
Laredo USA 35 G7
Larisa Greece 79 E3
Larnaca Cyprus 105 E7
Las Vegas USA 34 D3
Latvia (Country) 80 D4
Lausanne Switzerland 68 B6
Laval Canada 25 E7
Le Havre France 62 D2
Le Mans France 62 D3
Le Port Réunion 101 D6
Lebanon (Country) 106
Leeds UK 59 G5
Leeuwarden Netherlands 64 F2
Leeward Is. 43 H5
Leicester UK 59 G6
Leipzig Germany 67 G5
Lena (R.) Rus. Fed. 113 F4
León Mexico 39 E5
Leskovac Yugoslavia 77 C5
Lesotho (Country) 99 E7
Lesser Antilles (Is.) 43 G7
Lesser Sunda Is. Indonesia 127 E8
Lesvos (I.) Greece 79 G3
Lewis (I.) UK 58 D2

Lhasa China 118 D7
Liberia (Country) 92 D7
Libreville Gabon 95 B6
Libya (Country) 89
Libyan Desert Egypt 90 B4
Liechtenstein (Country) 68 D5
Liège Belgium 65 E6
Liepāja Latvia 80 B4
Ligurian Sea Italy 72 B4
Likasi Congo (Zaire) 95 G8
Lille France 63 E1
Lilongwe Malawi 97 E7
Lima Peru 45 B6
Limassol Cyprus 105 E7
Limnos (I.) Greece 79 F3
Limoges France 63 E5
Limpopo (R.) Mozambique/Southern Africa 99 E6/101 B6
Lincoln USA 33 G4
Linköping Sweden 57 D6
Linz Austria 69 F3
Lipari Is. Italy 73 F7
Lisbon Portugal 60 C5
Lithuania (Country) 81 C5
Little Rock USA 28 D3
Liverpool UK 59 F6
Ljubljana Slovenia 74 C4
Lobito Angola 98 A4
Loch Lomond UK 58 E4
Loch Ness UK 58 E3
Łodź Poland 71 E4
Lofoten Vesterålen (Is.) Norway 56 D3
Logrono Spain 61 F2
Loire (R.) France 62 D4
Lombardy Italy 72 C3
Lombok (I.) Indonesia 126 D8
Lomé Togo 93 E7
London Canada 24 D8
London UK 59 G7
Londonderry Northern Ireland UK 58 C4
Long Beach USA 37 D8/129 F3
Long I. USA 27 F6
Long Xuyen Vietnam 125 F6
Longyearbyen Svalbard Arctic Ocean 51 G7
Lopatka, Cape Rus. Fed. 113 H4
Los Àngeles Chile 49 B6
Los Angeles USA 37 D8
Louang Phrabang Laos 124 E4
Louisiana (State) USA 28 C5
Louisville USA 29 E2
Lower Tunguska Rus. Fed. 113 E5
Lualaba (R.) Congo (Zaire) 95 G6
Luanda Angola 98 A3
Luanshya Zambia 97 C6
Lubbock USA 35 F5
Lübeck Germany 66 E3
Lublin Poland 71 F4
Lubumbashi Congo (Zaire) 95 G8
Lucena Philippines 127 E2
Lucerne, Lake Switzerland 68 C5
Lucknow India 117 F3
Lüderitz Namibia 99 B6
Ludhiana India 117 E2
Luhans'k Ukraine 85 F4
Luoyang China 120 E4
Lusaka Zambia 97 C7
Luts'k Ukraine 84 C3
Luxembourg (Country) 65 F7
Luxor Egypt 90 D4
Luzon (I.) Philippines 127 E1
L'viv Ukraine 84 C3
Lyon France 63 F5

M
Maas (R.) W. Europe 64 F4
Maastricht Netherlands 65 E5
Macao 121 E6
Macdonnell Ranges (Mts.) Australia 132 D4
Macedonia (Country) 77
Maceió Brazil 47 H5
Mackenzie (R.) Canada 23 E5
Madagascar (Country) 101 C6
Madeira (Is.) Portugal 52 E4
Madeira (R.) Bolivia/Brazil 46 C4
Madison USA 31 E5
Madras India 100 E4/117 E7
Madrid Spain 61 E4
Madurai India 117 E7
Magadan Rus. Fed. 113 H4
Magdalena (R.) Colombia 44 B3
Magdeburg Germany 66 F4
Magellan, Strait of Chile 49 D8
Maggiore, Lake Italy 68 C6/72 B3
Mahilyow Belorussia 81 G6
Mai-Ndombe, Lake Congo (Zaire) 95 E6
Maine (State) USA 27 G2
Mainz Germany 67 D5
Majorca Balearic Is. Spain 61 H5
Makassar Strait Indonesia 127 E6

Makiyivka Ukraine 85 F4
Malabo Equatorial Guinea 95 B5
Málaga Spain 61 E7
Malang Indonesia 126 D8
Malatya Turkey 105 F5
Malawi (Country) 97
Malaysia (Country) 125
Malaysia (East) Borneo/ S.E. Asia 126 D5
Maldives (Country) 100 D4
Male Maldives 100 E4
Mali (Country) 93 E4
Malmo Sweden 57 C7
Malta (I.) 73 F8
Mamry, Lake Poland 71 F2
Man, Isle of UK 59 E5
Manado Indonesia 127 F5
Managua Nicaragua 42 B6
Manama Bahrain 109 F5
Manaus Brazil 46 D4
Manchester UK 59 F5
Manchuria China 120 G2
Mandalay Burma 124 C3
Mangalore India 117 E6
Manila Philippines 127 E2
Manisa Turkey 104 C5
Manitoba (Province) Canada 23 F7
Mannheim Germany 67 D6
Maputo (Mozambique) 99 F6
Mar del Plata Argentina 49 E5
Maracaibo Venezuela 44 C3
Marañón (R.) Peru 45 B5
Maribor Slovenia 74 D4
Mariupol' Ukraine 85 E4
Marmara, Sea of Turkey 104 C3
Maroua Cameroon 94 D4
Marquesas Is. France 129 F5
Marquette USA 31 F3
Marrakesh Morocco 88 D3
Marseilles France 63 F7
Marshall Is. (Country) 128 D4
Martinique France 43 H7
Maryland (State) USA 29 H2
Masai Steppe Tanzania 96 F4
Maseru Lesotho 99 E7
Mashhad Iran 109 H3
Massachusetts (State) USA 27 F5
Massif Central (Mts.) France 63 E6
Matadi Congo (Zaire) 95 D7
Maturín Venezuela 44 E3
Maun Botswana 99 D5
Mauritania (Country) 92 C4
Mauritius (Country) 101 D6
Mayotte (I.) France 101 C5
Mazār-e Sharīf Aghanistan 111 E5
Mazyr Belorussia 81 F7
Mbabane Swaziland 99 F6
Mbandaka Congo (Zaire) 95 E6
Mbeya Tanzania 97 E5
Mbuji-Mayi Congo (Zaire) 95 F7
Mead, Lake USA 34 D4
Mecca Saudi Arabia 108 D5
Medan Indonesia 126 A5
Medellín Colombia 44 B3
Mediterranean Sea 52 G4/ 61 F7/63/73/88/90 C2/ 104 /106 C4
Meerut India 117 E3
Mekong (R.) Asia 100 G3/ 119 E7/121 B5/124 D4/ 125 F6
Melaka Malaysia 125 E8
Melbourne Australia 133 F7
Melville I. Canada 23 E3/ 51 F4
Memphis USA 28 D3
Mendoza Argentina 49 B5
Mérida Mexico 39 H6
Mérida Venezuela 44 C3
Mersin Turkey 105 E6
Mesa USA 34 D5
Messina Sicily 73 F7
Messina, Strait of Italy 73 G7
Mestre Italy 72 D3
Meta (R.) Colombia/ Venezuela 44 C4
Meuse (R.) Western Europe 65 D6
Mexicali Mexico 38 D1
Mexico (Country) 38 – 39
Mexico, Gulf of USA 29 E6
Mexico City Mexico 39 F6
Michigan (State) USA 31 F3
Michigan, Lake USA 31 F4
Micronesia, Federated States of (Country) 128 D4
Middleburg Netherlands 64 C4
Midway Is. USA 129 E3
Milan Italy 72 C3
Milos (I.) Greece 79 F6
Milwaukee USA 31 F5
Minbu Burma 124 B4
Mindano (I.) Philippines 127 F4
Mindoro (I.) Philippines 127 E2
Minho (R.) Portugal 60 C2
Minneapolis USA 30 D4
Minnesota (State) 30 D2

Minorca Balearic Is. Spain 61 H4
Minsk Belorussia 81 E6
Miskolc Hungary 75 F2
Mississippi (R.) USA 28 D3/30 D3
Mississippi (State) USA 28 D4
Missouri (R.) USA 33 E2
Missouri (State) USA 33 H5
Mitumba Mts. Congo (Zaire) 95 G7
Mobile USA 28 D5
Mogadishu Somalia 91 G7
Mojave Desert USA 37 E7
Moldavia (Country) 84
Molucca Sea Indonesia 127 F5
Moluccas (Is.) Indonesia 127 F6
Mombasa Kenya 96 G4/101 C5
Monaco (Country) 63 G7
Mongolia (Country) 118 – 119
Monrovia Liberia 92 C7
Mons Belgium 65 C6
Montana (State) USA 32 D2
Monte Carlo Monaco 63 G7
Montenegro (Republic) Yugoslavia 77
Monterrey Mexico 39 F4
Montevideo Uruguay 49 E5
Montgomery USA 29 E4
Montpelier USA 27 F4
Montpellier France 63 F7
Montréal Canada 25 E7
Montserrat UK 43 H6
Monywa Burma 124 B3
Morava (R.) Czech Republic/Slovakia 70 D7
Moravia Czech Republic 70 D6
Morocco (Country) 88
Moroni Comoros 101 C5
Moscow Rus. Fed. 83 C5/112 C4
Mosel (R.) Germany 67 C6
Moselle (R.) France 63 G3
Mostar Bosnia & Herzegovina 75 E7
Mosul Iraq 109 E2
Moulmein Burma 125 C5
Moundou Chad 94 D4
Mozambique (Country) 98 – 99
Muang Phitsanulok Thailand 125 D5
Mufulira Zambia 97 C6
Mull (I.) UK 58 D3
Multan Pakistan 117 E2
Munich Germany 67 F7
Münster Germany 66 C4
Murcia Spain 61 F6
Murmansk Rus. Fed. 52 G3/82 D3/112 D3
Murray (R.) Australia 133 E6
Murrumbidgee (R.) Australia 133 F6
Muscat Oman 109 G6
Mwanza Tanzania 96 E4
Mweru, Lake Zambia/Congo (Zaire) 97 C5
Mykolayiv Ukraine 84 D4

N

Naberezhnyye Chelny Rus. Fed. 83 E6/112 C5
Nacala Mozambique 98 H4
Naga Philippines 127 E2
Nagoya Japan 123 D5
Nagpur India 117 E4
Nain Canada 25 F3
Nairobi Kenya 96 F4
Nakhodka Rus. Fed. 113 E4
Nakhon Ratchasima Thailand 125 E5
Nakhon Sawan Thailand 125 E5
Nakhon Si Thammarat Thailand 125 D7
Nam Dinh Vietnam 124 F4
Namangan Uzbekistan 111 F3
Namibe Angola 98 A4
Namibia (Country) 99
Namp'o North Korea 120 G3
Nampula Mozambique 98 H4
Namur Belgium 65 D6
Nanchang China 121 E5
Nancy France 63 F2
Nanjing China 120 F4
Nanning China 121 D6
Nantes France 62 D4
Napier NZ 134 G4
Naples Italy 73 F6
Narsarsuaq Greenland 51 E8
Nashville USA 29 E3
Nasik India 117 E5
Nassau Bahamas 43 E2
Nasser, Lake Egypt 90 D4
Natal Brazil 46 H4
Nauru (Country) 128 D4
Navarin, Cape Rus. Fed. 113 H2
Navoi Uzbekistan 111 E3
Naxos (I.) Greece 79 F6
N'djamena Chad 94 D4
Ndola Zambia 97 C6
Nebit Dag Turkmenistan 110 C3
Nebraska (State) USA 33 F4
Negro (R.) Brazil 46 C4

Negros (I.) Philippines 127 E3
Nepal (Country) 117 F3
Netherlands (Country) 64
Netherlands Antilles 43 F7
Neuchâtel, Lake Switzerland 68 B5
Nevada (State) USA 34 C2
New Amsterdam Guyana 44 G4
New Brunswick (Province) Canada 25 F6
New Caledonia (I.) France 128 D5
New Dehli India 117 E3
New Guinea (I.) 133 G1
New Hampshire (State) USA 27 E4
New Haven USA 27 F5
New Jersey (State) USA 27 F6
New Mexico (State) USA 35 F5
New Orleans USA 28 D5/32 B4
New South Wales (State) Australia 133 F5
New York (State) USA 27 E5
New York City USA 27 F6/52 B4
New Zealand (Country) 129 E6/134 – 135
Newark (New Jersey) USA 27 E7
Newark (New York State) USA 27 F6
Newcastle Australia 133 F6
Newfoundland (I.) Canada 25 G5
Newfoundland (Province) Canada 25 G4/52 C4
Newport USA 36 A4
Niagara Falls Canada/USA 24 D8/26 D4
Niamey Niger 93 F5
Nicaragua (Country) 42 C5
Nice France 63 G7
Nicobar Is. India 100 F4
Nicosia Cyprus 105 E7
Niedere Tauern (Mts.) Austria 69 F4
Niger (Country) 93 G4
Niger (R.) West Africa 53 F5/92 E4
Nigeria (Country) 93 G6
Nijmegen Netherlands 64 F4
Nile (R.) Egypt 91 C5/100 D3
Ningbo China 120 G4
Niš Yugoslavia 77 C5
Niue (I.) NZ 129 E5
Nizhniy Novgorod Rus. Fed. 83 D5
Nkongsamba Cameroon 95 C5
Nogales Mexico 38 D2
Nordfjord Norway 57 A5
Norfolk USA 29 H3
Noril'sk Rus. Fed. 113 E4
Normandy France 62 D3
Norrköping Sweden 57 D6
North Albanian Alps (Mts.) Albania 77 B5
North Cape Norway 56 F2
North Carolina (State) USA 29 G3
North Dakota (State) USA 33 F2
North I. NZ 134 E3
North Korea (Country) 120 G3
North Pole 51
North Sea 52 F3/59/64
Northern Ireland UK 59 C5
Northern Marianas Is. USA 128 D3
Northern Territory (State) Australia 132 D3
Northwest Territories (Province) Canada 23 E5
Norway (Country) 56 – 57
Norwegian Sea 56 C4
Nottingham UK 59 G6
Nouakchott Mauritania 92 C4
Nova Scotia (Province) Canada 25 F7
Novgorod Rus. Fed. 112 C3
Novi Sad Yugoslavia 76 B4
Novokuznetsk Rus. Fed. 113 E6
Novosibirsk Rus. Fed. 113 E6
Nubian Desert Sudan 90 D4
Nukus Uzbekistan 110 D2
Nullarbor Plain Australia 132 D5
Nuremburg Germany 67 F6
Nyasa, Lake Southern Africa 97 E6/98 G4

O

Oakland USA 37 B6
Oaxaca Mexico 39 F7
Ob' (R.) Rus. Fed. 113 E5
Odense Denmark 57 B7
Oder (R.) Germany 66 H3
Odesa Ukraine 84 D5
Odra (R.) C. Europe 70 C3
Ogbomosho Nigeria 93 F6
Ohio (R.) USA 31 G7
Ohio (State) USA 31 G6

Ohrid, Lake Albania/ Macedonia 77 C7
Okayama Japan 123 C5
Okhotsk, Sea of Japan 113 H4/122 F1/128 D2
Okinawa (I.) Japan 123 A8
Oklahoma (State) USA 33 G7
Oklahoma City USA 33 G7
Olenëk Bay Rus. Fed. 113 F3
Olympia USA 36 B3
Omaha USA 33 G4
Oman (Country) 109 G7
Oman, Gulf of 109 G6
Omdurman Sudan 91 D5
Omsk Rus. Fed. 112 D6
Onega (R.) Rus. Fed. 82 D4
Onega, Lake Rus. Fed. 82 C4
Onitsha Nigeria 93 F7
Ontario (Province) Canada 24 C5
Ontario, Lake Canada/ USA 24 D8/ 27 E4
Oran Algeria 89 E2
Orange (R.) Southern Africa 99 C7
Ordos Desert China 119 F5
Örebro Sweden 57 D6
Oregon (State) USA 36 C4
Orenburg Rus. Fed. 83 E6/112 C5
Orinoco (R.) Venezuela 44 E3
Orkney Is. UK 58 F2
Orlando USA 29 F6
Orléans France 63 E3
Orsha Belorussia 81 G5
Oruro Bolivia 45 D7
Ôsaka Japan 123 D5
Osh Kyrgyzstan 111 G3
Oshogbo Nigeria 93 F7
Osijek Croatia 75 E5
Oslo Norway 57 B6
Osorno Chile 49 B6
Ostrava Czech Republic 71 E6
Ottawa (R.) Canada 24 D7
Ottawa Canada 25 E7
Ou Mts. Japan 122 F3
Ouagadougou Burkina 93 E5
Ouargla Algeria 89 E3
Oujda Morocco 89 E2
Oulu Finland 56 F4
Outer Hebrides UK 58 D2
Oviedo Spain 60 D2
Oxnard USA 37 D8
Ozark Plateau USA 33 H6

P

Pacific Ocean 22/ 122–123/127/128–129
Padang Indonesia 126 B6
Padua Italy 72 D3
Painted Desert USA 35 E4
Pakistan (Country) 116 – 117
Pakokku Burma 124 B4
Pakxé Laos 125 F5
Palau (I.) USA 128 D4
Palawan (I.) Philippines 127 E3
Palembang Indonesia 126 B7
Palermo Sicily Italy 73 E7
Palma de Mallorca Majorca 61 H5
Palmer Land Antarctica 50 B4
Palu Indonesia 127 E6
Pamirs (Mts.) Tajikistan 111 G4
Pamplona Spain 61 F2
Pamukkale Turkey 104 D5
Panâevo Yugoslavia 74 F4
Panaji India 117 E6
Panama (Country) 42 D7
Panama Canal Panama 42 D7
Panama City Panama 42 D7/53 B5/129 H4
Panay (I.) Philippines 127 E3
Panevèžys Lithuania 81 D5
Papua New Guinea (Country) 133 G2
Paraguay (Country) 48 D3
Paraguay (R.) Paraguay 48 E3
Paramaribo Surinam 44 G4
Paraná (R.) S. America 47 E6/49 D5
Paraná Argentina 48 D4
Paris France 63 E3
Paros (I.) Greece 79 F6
Pasadena USA 35 H6/ 37 D8
Patagonia Argentina 49 C7
Paterson USA 27 F6
Patna India 117 F4
Patos Lagoon Brazil 47 E7
Patrai, Gulf of Greece 78 D5
Peá Yugoslavia 77 B5
Pécs Hungary 75 E4
Pegu Burma 125 C5
Peipus, Lake Estonia 80 E3
Peking China 120 E3
Pelagie Is. Italy 73 D8
Peloponne Greece 78 D5
Pennines UK 59 F5
Pennsylvania (State) USA 26 D6
Penza Rus. Fed. 83 C6/

112 C5
Peoria USA 31 E6
Perm' Rus. Fed. 83 E5/ 112 D5
Persian Gulf 100 D3/ 109 F4
Perth Australia 132 B6
Peru (Country) 45 B6
Peshawar Pakistan 117 E1
Petra Jordan 107 C6
Petropavlovsk-Kamchatskiy Rus. Fed. 113 H4
Philadelphia USA 27 E7
Philae Egypt 90 D4
Philippines (Country) 127
Phnom Penh Cambodia 125 F6
Phoenix USA 34 D5
Phuket (I.) Thailand 125 C7
Piatra-Neamţ Romania 76 F3
Pierre USA 33 F3
Pietermaritzburg South Africa 99 F7
Pilcomayo (R.) Bolivia/ Paraguay 48 D3
Pinang Malaysia 125 D7
Pindus Mts. Greece 78 D3
Pinsk Belorussia 81 D7
Piraeus Greece 79 E5
Pitcairn Is. UK 129 F5
Piteşti Romania 76 E4
Pittsburgh USA 26 D6
Piura Peru 45 A5
Plate (R.) Argentina/ Uruguay 49 E5
Pleven Bulgaria 77 E5
Ploieşti Romania 76 F4
Plovdiv Bulgaria 77 E5
Plymouth UK 59 E7
Plzeň Czech Republic 70 C6
Po (R.) Italy 72 D3
Podgorica Yugoslavia 77 A5
Podlasie Poland 71 F3
Pointe-Noire Congo 95 C7
Poitiers France 62 D5
Poland (Country) 70 – 71
Polynesia Pacific Ocean 129 F5
Pontianak Indonesia 126 C6
Port Elizabeth South Africa 99 D7
Port Harcourt Nigeria 93 F7
Port Louis Mauritius 101 D6
Port Moresby Papua New Guinea 133 G2
Port of Spain Trinidad 43 H8
Port Said Egypt 52 H4/90 D3/100 B3
Port Sudan Sudan 91 E5
Port-au-Prince Haiti 43 F5
Port-Gentil Gabon 95 B6
Portland USA 36 B3
Porto Portugal 60 C3
Pôrto Alegre Brazil 47 E7
Porto-Novo Benin 93 F7
Portugal (Country) 60
Posadas Argentina 48 E4
Potsdam Germany 66 G4
Powell, Lake USA 35 E3
Poza Rica Mexico 39 F6
Poznań Poland 70 D3
Prague Czech Republic 70 C5
Prespa, Lake S.E. Europe 77 G7
Pretoria South Africa 99 E6
Priština Yugoslavia 77 B5
Prince Edward I. (Province) Canada 25 F6
Prince of Wales I. Canada 23 F3
Prizren Yugoslavia 77 B5
Prome Burma 124 B4
Provence France 63 G7
Providence USA 27 F5
Prudhoe Bay Alaska USA 22 D3
Pskov Rus. Fed. 112 C3
Puebla Mexico 30 F6
Puerto Montt Chile 49 B6
Puerto Rico USA 43 G5
Puerto Santa Cruz Argentina 49 D8
Pune India 117 E5
Punta Arenas Chile 49 C8
Purus (R.) Brazil/Peru 46 C4
Pusan South Korea 120 H3
Putorana Mts. Rus. Fed. 113 E4
Putumayo (R.) Peru 45 C5
Pyinmana Burma 124 C4
Pyongyang North Korea 120 G3
Pyrénées (Mts.) S.W. Europe 61 G2/62 D8

Q
Qandahār Afghanistan 111 E7
Qatar (Country) 109 F5
Qena Egypt 90 D4
Qingdao China 120 F3
Qinghai China 119 E6
Qiqihar China 120 F2
Qondūz (R.) Afghanistan 111 F5
Québec (Province) Canada 25 E5
Queensland (State) Australia 133 F4

Qui Nhon Vietnam 125 G5
Quito Ecuador 45 A5

R
Rabat Morocco 88 D2
Rach Gia Vietnam 125 F6
Rajkot India 116 D4
Rajshahi Bangladesh 117 G4
Raleigh USA 29 G3
Râmnicu Vâlcea Romania 76 D4
Ranchi India 117 F4
Rangoon Burma 100 F4/125 C5
Rasht Iran 109 F2
Rat Buri Thailand 125 D5
Rawalpindi Pakistan 117 E1
Recife Brazil 47 H5
Red (R.) China/Vietnam 124 E3
Red Sea 90 E4/100 C3/ 108 D5
Redding USA 37 B5
Regina Canada 23 F8
Reno USA 34 C2
Resistencia Argentina 48 E4
Reşiţa Romania 76 B4
Reykavik Iceland 52 E3
Rheims France 63 F2
Rhine (R.) W. Europe 64 F4/66 C7/68 C4
Rhode I. (State) USA 27 G5
Rhodes (I.) Greece 79 H7
Rhône (R.) W. Europe 63 F6/68 B6
Richmond USA 29 G2
Riga Latvia 80 D4
Riga, Gulf of Estonia/ Latvia 80 D4
Río Cuarto Argentina 49 C5
Rio de Janeiro Brazil 47 G6/52 D6
Río Grande (R.) Mexico 39 F3
Rio Grande USA 35 F6
Riverside USA 37 D8
Rivne Ukraine 84 C3
Riyadh Saudi Arabia 109 E5
Roanoke USA 29 G2
Rochester USA 27 E4
Rockford USA 31 E5
Rocky Mts. N. America 22 D6/35 E4
Romania (Country) 76
Rome Italy 73 D5
Rosario Argentina 49 D5
Rostock (Germany) 66 F3
Rostov-na-Donu Rus. Fed. 83 B6/112 B5
Rotterdam Netherlands 52 F4/64 D4
Rouen France 63 E2
Rovuma (R.) C. Africa 98 H4
Rub' al Khali Saudi Arabia 109 E7
Ruse Bulgaria 77 E5
Russian Federation (Country) 81 B5/ 82 – 83/ 112 – 113
Rwanda (Country) 96 D4
Ryazan' Rus. Fed. 83 C5/ 112 C4

S
Saarbrücken Germany 67 C6
Sabah Malaysia 126 D5
Sabhā Libya 89 G4
Sacramento USA 37 B6
Sagaing Burma 124 C3
Sahara (Desert) N. Africa 88 – 89/92 – 93
Sahel West Africa 93 E5
Sakhalin (I.) Rus. Fed. 112 H5
Salem USA 36 B4
Salt Lake City USA 34 D2
Salta Paraguay 48 C3
Salton Sea USA 37 E8
Salvador Brazil 47 H5
Salween (R.) Burma/ China 119 E7/121 B5/ 124 C4
Salzburg Austria 69 F3
Samar (I.) Philippines 127 F3
Samara Rus. Fed. 83 D6/112 C5
Samarinda Indonesia 126 D6
Samarkand Uzbekistan 111 E4
Sambre (R.) Belgium/ France 65 D6
Samos (I.) Greece 79 G5
Samsun Turkey 105 F3
San'a Yemen 109 E8
San Antonio USA 35 G7
San Bernardo Chile 49 B5
San Diego USA 37 D8
San Francisco USA 37 B6
San José Costa Rica 42 C7
San Jose USA 37 B7
San Juan Puerto Rico 43 G5
San Luis Potosí Mexico 39 F5
San Marino (Country) 72 D4
San Miguel de Tucumán Argentina 48 C4
San Salvador El Salvador

42 B5
San Salvador de Jujuy Paraguay 48 C3
Sanandaj Iran 109 F2
Sandoway Burma 124 B4
Santa Ana USA 37 D8
Santa Barbara USA 37 C8
Santa Cruz Bolivia 45 E7
Santa Fe Argentina 48 D4
Santa Fe USA 35 F4
Santa Marta Colombia 44 B3
Santander Spain 61 E2
Santarém Brazil 46 E4
Santiago Chile 49 B5
Santiago de Compostela Spain 60 C2
Santo Domingo Dominican Rep. 43 F5
São Francisco (R.) Brazil 47 G5
São Luís Brazil 46 G4
São Paulo Brazil 47 F6
São Tomé & Príncipe (Country) 53 G5/95 B6
Saône (R.) France 63 F4
Sapporo Japan 122 F2
Sarajevo Bosnia & Herzegovina 75 E7
Saratov Rus. Fed. 83 C6/112 C5
Sarawak Malaysia 126 D5
Sardinia (I.) Italy 73 B6
Sargasso Sea 52
Sarh Chad 94 E4
Sarī Iran 109 G2
Saskatchewan (Province) Canada 23 F7
Saskatoon Canada 23 F7
Satu Mare Romania 76 D2
Saudi Arabia (Country) 109 E6
Sault Ste Marie Canada 24 C6/31 G3
Savannah USA 29 F5
Savannakhét Laos 125 F5
Saxony Germany 66 E3
Schwerin Germany 66 F3
Scilly, Isles of UK 59 C8
Scoresbysund Greenland 51 F8
Scotia Sea 50 B3/53 D7
Scotland UK 58
Seattle USA 36 B3/129 F2
Seine (R.) France 63 E2
Semarang Indonesia 126 C8
Semipalatinsk Kazakhstan 113 E6
Semnān Iran 109 G2
Sendai Japan 122 F4
Senegal (Country) 92 C4
Seoul South Korea 120 G3
Seram (I.) Indonesia 127 F6
Serbia (Republic) 76
Seremban Malaysia 125 E8
Sétif Algeria 89 E2
Setúbal Portugal 60 C6
Sevastopol' Ukraine 85 E5
Severn (R.) UK 59 F7
Severnaya Zemlya (Is.) Rus. Fed. 113 E2
Seville Spain 60 D7
Seychelles (Country) 101 D5
Sfax Tunisia 89 F3
Shanghai China 120 F4/128 C3
Shannon (R.) Ireland 59 B5
Shaoxing China 120 F4
Sheffield UK 59 G6
Shenyang China 120 G3
's-Hertogenbosch Netherlands 64 E4
Shetland Is. UK 58 G1
Shijiazhuang China 120 E3
Shikoku (I.) Japan 123 C6
Shíráz Iran 109 F4
Sholapur India 117 E5
Shreveport USA 28 C4
Shumen Bulgaria 77 F5
Shymkent Kazakhstan 112 D7
Šiauliai Lithuania 81 C5
Siberia Rus. Fed. 113 E5
Sibiu Romania 76 D4
Sicily (I.) Italy 73 E7
Sidi Bel Abbès Algeria 89 E2
Sierra Leone (Country) 92 C6
Sierra Madre (Mts.) Mexico 38 D3/39
Sierra Nevada (Mts.) Spain 61 E7
Sierra Nevada USA 37 C6
Silesia Czech Republic/Poland 70 D5
Simbirsk Rus. Fed. 83 D6/112 C5
Simferopol' Ukraine 85 E5
Simpson Desert Australia 133 E4
Sinai (Peninsula) Egypt 90 D3
Singapore (Country) 125 E8
Sinŭiju North Korea 120 G3
Sittang (R.) Burma 124 C4
Sivas Turkey 105 F4
Skiros (I.) Greece 79 F4
Skopje Macedonia 77 C5
Skye (I.) UK 58 D3
Sliven Bulgaria 77 F5
Slovakia (Country) 71
Slovenia (Country) 74

Smederevo Yugoslavia 76 G4
Smolensk Rus. Fed. 112 C4
Socotra (I.) Yemen 100 D4
Sofia Bulgaria 77 D6
Sohâg Egypt 90 C4
Solomon Is. (Country) 128 D5
Somalia (Country) 91
Songkhla Thailand 125 D7
Sosnowiec Poland 71 E5
South Africa (Country) 99
South Australia (State) Australia 133 E5
South Carolina (State) USA 29 F4
South China Sea S.E. Asia 100 G4/121 E6/125 G6/126 C4
South Dakota (State) USA 33 F3
South Georgia (I.) UK 53 D7
South I. NZ 135 D7
South Korea (Country) 120 H3
South Pole Antarctica 50 C5
South Sandwich Is. UK 53 E7
Southampton I. Canada 23 G5
Southern Alps (Mts.) NZ 135 C6
Southern Ocean 128–129
Soweto South Africa 99 E6
Spain (Country) 60 – 61
Spitsbergen (I.) Norway 51 G7
Split Croatia 74 D7
Sporades (Is.) Greece 79 E3
Springfield USA 27 F5/31 E7/33 H6
Sri Lanka (Country) 100 E4/117 F8
Srinagar India 117 E1
St. Étienne France 63 F5
St. Helena (I.) UK 53 E6
St. John's Canada 25 H5
St. Kitts and Nevis (Country) 43 H6
St. Lawrence (R.) Canada 25 F6
St. Lawrence Seaway Canada 25 E7/52 B4
St. Lawrence, Gulf of Canada 25 F5
St. Louis USA 33 H5
St. Lucia (Country) 43 H7
St. Paul USA 30 D4
St. Petersburg Rus. Fed. 82 B4/112 C3
St. Petersburg USA 29 F7
St. Pierre & Miquelon France 25 G6
St. Polten Austria 69 G2
St. Vincent and The Grenadines (Country) 43 H7
Stara Zagora Bulgaria 77 D5
Stewart I. NZ 135 B8
Stockholm Sweden 57 D6
Stockton USA 37 B6
Stony Tunguska Rus. Fed. 113 F5
Strasbourg France 63 G2
Stromboli (I.) Italy 73 F7
Stuttgart Germany 67 D6
Suceava Romania 76 E3
Sucre Bolivia 45 E8
Sudan (Country) 91
Sudbury Canada 24 D7
Sudeten Mts. Czech Republic/Poland 70 D5
Suez Canal Egypt 100 B3
Suez, Gulf of S.W. Asia 90 D3
Sula Is. Indonesia 127 F6
Sulu Archipelago (Is.) Philippines 127 E4
Sumatra (I.) Indonesia 101 G5/126 B6
Sumba (I.) Indonesia 127 E8
Sumbawa (I.) Indonesia 127 E8
Sumy Ukraine 85 E3
Superior, Lake Canada/USA 24 C6/31 F2
Surabaya Indonesia 126 D8
Surat India 117 E5
Surinam (Country) 44 G4
Svalbard (Is.) Norway 51 G5
Swaziland (Country) 99 F6
Sweden (Country) 56 – 57
Switzerland (Country) 68
Sydney Australia 128 D6/133 F6
Syracuse USA 27 E4
Syria (Country) 106
Syrian Desert Middle East 107 E5/109 E3

T
Tabora Tanzania 97 E5
Tacloban Philippines 127 F3
Tacna Peru 45 C7
Tacoma USA 36 B3
Taegu South Korea 120 H3
Tagus (R.) Spain 60 D3
Tahiti (I.) France 129 F5

Tahoe, Lake USA 34 C2/ 37 C6
Taipei Taiwan 121 G5
Taiping Malaysia 125 D8
Taiwan (Country) 121 G5
Taiwan Strait 121 F5
Taiyuan China 120 E3
Talcahuano Chile 49 B6
Tallahassee USA 29 E5
Tallinn Estonia 80 D3
Tamanrasset Algeria 89 E6
Tampa USA 29 F7
Tampere Finland 57 F5
Tanganyika, Lake C. Africa 95 H7/97 D5
Tanggula Mts. China 118 D6
Tangier Morocco 88 D2
Tangshan China 120 F3
Tanjungkarang Indonesia 120 C7
Tanzania (Country) 96 – 97
Tapachula Mexico 39 G8
Tapajós (R.) Brazil 46 D4
Taranto Italy 73 G6
Târgovişte Romania 76 E4
Târgu Mureş 76 C3
Tartu Estonia 80 E3
Tashauz Turkmenistan 110 D3
Tashkent Uzbekistan 111 F3
Tasman Sea 128 D6/ 133 F7/135 F4
Tasmania (State) Australia 133 E7
Taunggyi Burma 124 C4
Taupo, Lake NZ 134 F4
Taurus Mts. Turkey 105 E6
Tavoy Burma 125 C5
Tbilisi Georgia 85 G7
Tegucigalpa Honduras 42 B5
Tehran Iran 109 G2
Tel Aviv-Yafo Israel 107 C5
Temuco Chile 49 B6
Tennessee (R.) USA 29 E2
Tennessee (State) USA 29 E3
Teresina Brazil 46 G4
Ternopil' Ukraine 84 C3
Tetovo Macedonia 77 B5
Texas (State) USA 35 G6
Thai Nguyen Vietnam 124 F4
Thailand (Country) 124–125
Thames (R.) UK 59 F7
Thane India 117 E5
Thanh Hoa Vietnam 124 F4
Thaton Burma 125 C5
Thessaloniki Greece 79 E2
Thimphu Bhutan 117 G3
Thule Greenland 51 F6
Thunder Bay Canada 24 C6
Tibetan Autonomous Region China 118 C6
Tientsin China 120 E3
Tierra del Fuego (I.) Argentina/Chile 49 D8
Tigris (R.) S.W. Asia 105 G5/106 H2/109 E2
Tijuana Mexico 38 C1
Timbuktu Mali 93 E4
Timmins Canada 24 D6
Timor (I.) Indonesia 127 F8
Tirana Albania 77 A6
Tobago (I.) 43 H8
Togo (Country) 93 E6
Tokelau (Is.) NZ 129 E5
Tokyo Japan 123 F5
Toledo Spain 61 E5
Toledo USA 31 G5
Tol'yatti Rus. Fed. 83 D6/ 112 C5
Tomsk Rus. Fed. 113 E6
Tonga (Country) 129 E5
Tongking, Gulf of China/ Vietnam 121 D6/124 G4
Topeka USA 33 G5
Toronto Canada 24 D7
Toulouse France 63 E7
Trabzon Turkey 105 G3
Transantarctic Mts. Antarctica 50 C5
Trenton USA 27 E6
Trieste Italy 72 E3
Trinidad (I.) 43 H8
Trinidad and Tobago (Country) 43 H8
Tripoli Lebanon 106 D4
Tripoli Libya 89 F3
Tristan da Cunha (I.) UK 53 F7
Trivandrum India 117 E8
Trondheim Norway 57 C5
Trujillo Peru 45 A6
Tuamotu Archipelago (Is.) France 129 F5
Tucson USA 34 D5
Tulsa USA 33 G6
Tunis Tunisia 89 F2
Tunisia (Country) 89 F3
Turin Italy 72 B3
Turk and Caicos Is. UK 43 F4
Turkana, Lake Ethiopia/ Kenya 91 E7/96 F3
Turkey (Country) 104–105
Turkmenistan (Country)

110 – 111
Turku Finland 57 F6
Tuvalu (Country) 129 E5
Tuzla Bosnia & Herzegovina 75 E6

U
Ubon Ratchathani Thailand 125 F5
Udon Thani Thailand 125 E5
Ufa Rus. Fed. 83 E6/112 C5
Uganda (Country) 96
Ujung Pandang Indonesia 127 E7
Ukraine (Country) 84–85
Ulan Bator Mongolia 119 F3
Ulan-Ude Rus. Fed. 113 F6
United Arab Emirates (Country) 109 F6
United Kingdom (Country) 58 – 59
United States of America (Country) 22 – 37
Uppsala Sweden 57 D6
Ural Mts. Rus. Fed. 83 F5/112
Ural'sk Rus. Fed. 112 C5
Urgench Uzbekistan 110 D3
Uruguay (Country) 48–49
Ürümqi China 118 D4
Utah (State) USA 34 D2
Utrecht Netherlands 64 E4
Uzbekistan (Country) 110 – 111

V
Vaasa Finland 57 E5
Vadodara India 117 E4
Vaduz Liechtenstein 68 D5
Valdivia Chile 49 B6
Valencia Spain 61 F5
Valencia Venezuela 44 D3
Valladolid Spain 61 F3
Valletta Malta 73 F8
Valparáiso Chile 49 B5/ 129 H6
Van Turkey 104 H5
Vanadzor Armenia 85 G7
Vancouver Canada 22 D8/ 129 F2
Vancouver I. Canada 22 D8
Vaner, Lake Sweden 57 C6
Vanuatu (Country) 128 D5
Varanasi India 117 F4
Vardar (R.) Greece/ Macedonia 77 C6
Varna Bulgaria 77 F5
Västerås Sweden 57 D6
Vatican City (Vatican City State) Italy 73 D5
Vatter, Lake Sweden 57 C6
Venezuela (Country) 44 D3
Venezuela, Gulf of 44 D3
Venice Italy 72 D3
Venice, Gulf of Italy 72 E3
Verkhoyansk Range (Mts.) Rus. Fed. 113 G4
Vermont (State) USA 27 F4
Verona Italy 72 D3
Victoria (State) Australia 133 F6
Victoria Canada 22 D8
Victoria Seychelles 100 D5
Victoria Falls Zambia 97 B7
Victoria Falls Zambia/ Zimbabwe 99 E5
Victoria I. Canada 23 E4
Victoria, Lake E. Africa 96 E4
Vienna Austria 69 H2
Vientiane Laos 124 E4
Viet Tri Vietnam 124 F4
Vietnam (Country) 124 – 125
Vijayawada India 117 F6
Villahermosa Mexico 39 G7
Villavicencio Colombia 44 B4
Vilnius Lithuania 81 D5
Viña del Mar Chile 49 B5
Vinh Vietnam 124 F4
Vinnytsya Ukraine 84 D3
Virgin Is. US 43 G5
Virginia (State) USA 29 G2
Vishakhapatnam India 117 F5
Vistula (R.) Poland 71 F5
Vitoria Spain 61 F2
Vitsyebsk N.E. Europe 81 G5
Vladivostok Rus. Fed. 113 H7
Vlorë Albania 77 B6
Volga (R.) Rus. Fed. 83 D6
Volgograd Rus. Fed. 83 C6/112 C5
Volta, Lake Ghana 93 E7
Vorkuta Russia 82 G4
Voronezh Rus. Fed. 83 B6/112 C5

W
Wabash (R.) USA 31 F6
Waco USA 35 G6
Wad Medani Sudan 91 D5
Waddenzee Netherlands 64 E2
Wairau (R.) NZ 135 E5

Wales UK 59
Walla Walla USA 36 D3
Wallis & Futuna (Is.) France 129 E5
Walvis Bay Namibia 99 B6
Warsaw Poland 71 E4
Warta (R.) Poland 71 D3
Washington (State) USA 36 C3
Washington D.C. USA 29 G2
Waterbury USA 27 F5
Weddell Sea Antarctica 50 B4/53 D8
Wellington NZ 129 E6/135 F5
West Bank 107 C5
West Virginia (State) USA 29 F2
Western Australia (State) Australia 132 C4
Western Sahara (Country) 88
Western Samoa (Country) 129 E5
Westport NZ 135 D5
White Sea Rus. Fed. 82 D4
Whitehorse Canada 22 D5
Wichita USA 33 G6
Wiesbaden Germany 67 D5
Wight, Isle of UK 59 F7
Wilmington USA 27 E7
Windhoek Namibia 99 B6
Windsor Canada 24 C8
Windward Is. 43 H7
Winnebago, Lake USA 31 F4
Winnipeg Canada 23 F8
Winston-Salem USA 29 G3
Winterthur Switzerland 68 C4
Wisconsin (R.) USA 31 E5
Wisconsin (State) USA 31 E3
Wollongong Australia 133 F6
Wolverhampton UK 59 F6
Woods, Lake of the Canada/USA 24 B5/30 D1
Worcester USA 27 F5
Wrangel I. Rus. Fed. 51 G2/113 G1
Wrocław Poland 70 D5
Wuhan China 120 E4
Wyoming (State) USA 33 E4

X
Xi'an China 120 D4
Xiamen China 121 F5
Xingu (R.) Brazil 46 E4
Xining China 119 E5
Xinjiang Ulghur Autonomous Region of China 118 C4

Y
Yakutsk Rus. Fed. 113 G4
Yamoussoukro Ivory Coast 92 D7
Yangtze (R.) China 120 D4
Yaoundé Cameroon 95 C3
Yarlung Zangbo (see Brahmaputra)
Yaroslavl' Rus. Fed. 83 C5/112 C4
Yāsūj Iran 109 F4
Yazd Iran 109 G3
Yekaterinburg Rus. Fed. 112 C5
Yellow Sea China 120 F3
Yellowknife Canada 23 E5
Yemen (Country) 109 E8
Yenisey (R.) Rus. Fed. 113 E5
Yerevan Armenia 85 G7
Yogyakarta Indonesia 126 C8
Yokohama Japan 123 F5/128 D3
Yucatán Peninsula Mexico 39 H6
Yugoslavia (Country) 77
Yukon (R.) Canada/USA 22 C4/129 E1
Yukon Territory (Province) Canada 22 D4

Z
Zadar Croatia 74 C6
Zagreb Croatia 74 D3
Zagros Mts. Iran 109 G4
Zāhedān Iran 109 H4
Zaire, also Congo (Zaire) (Country) 95 F6
Zambezi (R.) Southern Africa 97 B7/97 B7/101 B5
Zambia (Country) 97
Zamboanga Philippines 127 E4
Zanjān Iran 109 F2
Zanzibar Tanzania 97 G5
Zanzibar (I.) Tanzania 97 G5
Zaozhuang China 120 F4
Zaporizhzhya Ukraine 85 E4
Zaragoza Spain 61 F3
Zenica Bosnia & Herzegovina 75 E6
Zhengzhou China 120 E4
Zhytomyr Ukraine 84 D3
Zimbabwe (Country) 99
Zonguldak Turkey 104 D3
Zurich Switzerland 68 C5
Zurich, Lake Switzerland 68 C5
Zwolle Netherlands 64 F3